T0365783

THE EDGE

*An emotional journey through a life filled with
love, loss, grief, anger, joy and autism.*

SONIA FACEY

Copyright © 2015 by Sonia Facey. 727546

ISBN: Softcover   978-1-5144-4188-6
        Hardcover   978-1-5144-4189-3
        EBook   978-1-5144-4187-9

All rights reserved. No part of this book may
be reproduced or transmitted in any form or by
any means, electronic or mechanical, including
photocopying, recording, or by any information storage
and retrieval system, without permission in writing from
the copyright owner.

Print information available on the last page

Rev. date: 11/10/2015

To order additional copies of this book, contact:
Xlibris
1-800-455-039
www.xlibris.com.au
Orders@Xlibris.com.au

Contents

DEDICATION

To all the amazing teachers and aides who have worked with Nathan over the years I want to say a special Thank You for the work you do in caring for all our special children. Working with Nathan is never easy and your care, patience and dedication is truly inspiring.

I have many friends from many different walks of life and each and every one of you has a special place in my heart. Thank You to all those who have been there to support and guide me, been by my side as I have cried and cried with me but most of all for everyone who has laughed with me.

"If I had a flower for every time you made me smile or laugh,

I'd have a garden to walk in forever"

Thank You to Russell Edwards and Jade Aroha Tonta for your most valued editing skills and the suggestions you have offered to make my book the best it possibly can be.

To my amazing sons, Brendon and Josh you both deserve the hugest Thanks. You have been through so much with me but you are always there with a helping hand when things get tough or just when I am being technically challenged and can't work the TV or computer. I am so proud of the amazing young men that you have grown into.

To my youngest, Nathan, I have to say a huge Thanks for just being you. You have challenged me, taught me but most of all you have made me a better person.

To all my boys I love you with all of my heart.

To my sisters, who are always just a phone call away, though we don't live close you are always in my heart. Thank you for being my big sister's and best friends. To my brothers, who were my protectors as I grew up, Thank you for being there for me throughout our younger years.

The last Thanks and a very, very important one is for my Mum. You have cared, understood, loved us and are always there for me. Thank you for helping me see the dream of getting my book published. If it wasn't for you being the strong woman you have always been I would not have had the strength to make it through all the challenges that have come my way.

Thank You Mum, I love you.

PREFACE

Why would I want to write a book? So many people have asked me that. I decided to write "The Edge" because people only see small snippets of my life and can't understand how I cope with the challenges that I have had to face. My life has taken many twists and turns to get to where I am now and in writing "The Edge" I wanted to share what I have experienced along the way.

When I started writing this book I was going to say that you wouldn't find much hope within its pages but one of my motto's has always been *"Where there's life, there's hope"*. Even though my story is not an easy one there are glimmers of hope along this intense and turbulent journey.

I've heard it said that through adversity comes triumph. Well I have lived with more than my fair share of adversity with few triumphs. The main triumph I can take from living with a lot of adversity is that I am a much better, stronger person.

"The Edge" is not just another story about autism. It is my story about how I came, from humble beginnings as a shy country girl, to be living in the big smoke with an almost ex-husband, who I am trying to find a way to be friends with, and three wonderful sons, the youngest just happens to have autism.

"The Edge" is my story about living with adversity, living with a child with autism and the emotional and physical scarring that has occurred on this most difficult of journeys.

START OF THE JOURNEY

The start of my journey on this planet, of course, starts with my Mum and Dad who without them I wouldn't be here. Before I arrived my four siblings came before me, my eldest brother, Andrew, twin sisters Natalie and Michelle, and another brother, Craig and that makes me the baby of the family.

Sadly, my dad passed away when my eldest, Brendon, was only six weeks old. While he was on this earth he was the sweetest man and my best friend, but he had a dark side. This dark side was a mental illness that tormented him right throughout his adult life. Mum always thought his illness was brought on when he contracted mumps six weeks before they were married but with the prevalence of mental illness throughout our family she doesn't seem to think that anymore. She doesn't know what to believe now, but I think there may be several defective genes in our family line since two of my uncles were alcoholics while another committed suicide by jumping off the Brisbane Bridge.

There is a history of alcoholism, bipolar and anxiety disorder through my family. Whether it is genetic or we as a family had some sort of curse over us who is to say.

When Dad first went to hospital he was diagnosed with many things from schizophrenia to manic depression, but nowadays I think it would be diagnosed as bipolar.

Dad did some pretty strange, but funny things during his manic episodes. One time the police bought him home in nothing but his undies after he had gone swimming in the lake in the middle of the night. There was another time Mum found him escaping from the hospital with a banana in his hand which he told her he was going to trade at the shop for smokes.

Dad never used to smoke when he was first married. It wasn't until he went to hospital that he took up the habit. The ward staff thought that giving the psych patients cigarettes would be soothing for them and it would give them something to do. This all occurred before the side effects of smoking were ever fully known. Dad's habit continued, no matter how hard he tried to kick it, right up until his death.

The harsher side saw a man who didn't believe in swearing begin to swear compulsively, punch holes in walls and he hit me once in a car park in Canberra when I tried to get him to get back in the car to go back to my sister's house. When he realised how much he had upset me he kept trying to apologise but I didn't want to see him for a while. It took me a while to get over that but I knew he was seriously ill and he never meant to hurt me. I was always very wary of him after that.

When I got my licence, and Dad wasn't allowed to drive, I would take him out driving. On one of our outings he, all of a sudden, got cranky, reached across and tried to rip the keys out of the ignition. I had to punch him in the face to make him stop. If we were out on the highway I may not be here to write this book as we could have been wiped out by one of the many trucks that passed through Forbes. Thankfully we were on a quiet, back road and I was able to pull off the road safely.

One night I had to hide under the pool table because Dad was chasing Mum around the room with a knife. I can't remember who but someone ran outside to get my uncle, who was living in a caravan out the back, to come in and subdue him. That was one of the scariest things I had ever seen him do. Due to the severity of this incident there was no other choice but to send him back to be hospitalised.

The doctors at a hospital in North Sydney decided they were going to try electric shock therapy. I just happened to be right near the door as they wheeled him out of his first session. That had to be one of the most gut wrenching times in my young life. Even though my Dad had been mentally ill a lot of my life he was still strong and healthy but not this day. He couldn't speak, he was drooling and he could barely lift his hand off the bed. He didn't recognize us at first. I held his hand and the pain that was in his eyes was indescribable and even 20 years after his passing it still haunts me sometimes.

As he started to recognise his surroundings and us, tears came to his eyes. I didn't cry that day because it was like being in a dream, a horrible nightmare, and I didn't want my dad to see his pain reflected in my eyes. When I think about it now, I still get a little emotional because it must have been so hard for such a proud, wonderful man to succumb to such torture.

If my Dad were still alive and he hadn't been sick I could see us now running a farm together. He taught me so many things from looking after the animals, driving the forklift so I could feed them, how to fix a fence, how to kill a chicken and gut and pluck it for our dinner, he taught me to sharpen knives so I could help him cut up the meat after he had butchered the animals.

I was down the paddock with him one day when he was slaughtering a sheep and he threw some of the stomach contents to one of our dogs, Rusty. Rusty picked up some of the pieces and started to shake it around. I only realised what he had picked up after poo started flying everywhere. I only just managed to get out of the way to avoid being covered in sheep faeces. Dad couldn't stop laughing at me when he saw me running from the flying sheep poop.

When Dad was well he would never go crook on me. One day I asked him if I could borrow the car (I didn't have my licence at the time) to go down to the Cotton's Weir which was only a couple of kilometres from our house and he let me. I had a couple of friends with me and when we got there our other friends, who we were supposed to meet, weren't there so we decided to go to another part of the river to see if we could find them. In the meantime Mum had gotten a phone call to say she had to go into work so Dad walked down to the Weir to find us only to find that we weren't there. They had to ring a friend to come and take her to work. When I got home he never roused on me he just told me that he had walked down to find me and that Mum had to go to work. It was in the lack of words that I knew that I had done the wrong thing and I didn't do it again, not until I got my licence anyway.

Despite his illness he loved his family and his beautiful spirit is what my Mum loved so much about him, and why she fought so hard to get help for him.

My Mum was not always my best friend when I was growing up but she is now and, at times, it felt like she was my only friend. We didn't see eye to eye most of the time and being only little I couldn't understand why she wasn't around for us so much of the time. I was always a little sad when there were things on at school and other mums would be there with their kids and mine never was.

I was with my older sisters' a lot and I feel like I learnt more from them, than I did my mum. Now I am older I can understand why she wasn't around. For most of their marriage Mum was the one who had to be the money earner. When she wasn't working and was away with Dad at the hospital I know that she was trying to find a way to get help for Dad so the five of us kids could have our father around.

I look back at all the things my mum did to try to keep us together from running a second hand shop, a café and when we lived on the farm she never stopped working. She also went and did work for our neighbours. In the tomato season she would be working on the tomato picking machine.

Nat also worked with mum on the tomato picking machine but, unfortunately, for Nat she has always had motion sickness so with the smell of rotten tomatoes and the motion of the machine Nat was often rather ill. We would go over after school sometimes to see them working on that massive machine. We would climb up and help them sort through the tomatoes until they were able to come home with us.

Picking pumpkins was another job she took on which we helped her with a couple of times. What an awful job that was. You ended up so prickly and itchy. There was certainly no fighting as to who was going to have a bath on those days.

The favourite job but one of the hardest was felling trees to clear paddocks, for farmers to plant crops. It was the best job because once they had been cut down all the wood would be piled up and all the neighbours would come around and bring fireworks and we would have a huge party.

There was one very important thing that I learned from my mother and that is to be strong. If she wasn't the strong person that she is we would probably have ended up in foster homes.

Dad sneaking in a bit of a smooch

My first school photo

I Had A Dream

Last night I had a dream
Peaceful music, beautiful soft clouds
Beside a magnificent grand piano you sat
No more pain was in your heart
For you were in your rightful home

Twenty years on you are still missed
Your life on earth was troubled
Although tortured by your past
you were loved by many
Five kids, wife, family, friends
Knowing you are finally at peace
negates the regret of words not said

Although taken from us too soon
The pain is gone from your soul
Free from the chains that held you down
With our Creator, among the clouds,
you now abound
Lifted to eternal peace, by the angels above
to your heavenly home on wings of love

by Sonia Facey

HUMBLE BEGINNINGS

I was born at Albury Base Hospital in 1971 but I was only a baby when we moved to our farm at Grenfell. This farm was a land of wonder and excitement for me with great gardens, paddocks and loads and loads of animals. Being the youngest of five kids I got to enjoy the best of both worlds because when my four siblings were at school I got to spend some really great times with my Mum and Dad. As they would head off to school I would head off with Mum and Dad to help around the farm. My fondest memory of those times was helping in the shearing sheds. I felt very special as I got to drink tea and eat bickies with Dad and all the shearers. Even to this day sometimes when I smell a cup of tea those memories come flooding back to me.

Other times when my sisters and brothers were home we were hardly ever indoors. We were always off doing something like playing hide and seek in the hay stacks, building cubby houses, climbing trees and swimming in the dams. We always had amazing adventures, as we headed off up to into the Weddin Mountains behind our farm, and would go roaming through the bush and exploring the caves. At the entrance to one of the caves we used to play in we found a plaque which said that Ben Hall had once used it at his hide out. Many years later when I learnt about bushrangers I realised just how truly cool that place had been.

A bushfire once swept through the Weddin Mountains. Mum and Dad went to help fight the fire and we were sent to safety at our neighbour's place. We stood up on the brick wall that surrounded their large cactus garden and watched as the flames came over the mountain heading toward our property. The fire ripped through the mountain but it didn't jump the road and our property was safe. We were mucking around up on the wall as well and I slipped into the garden. I ended up with prickles all up my arms, legs and in my butt. Mum spent days digging out those horrible prickles.

For the most part I loved being a part of a big family but sometimes my siblings could really give me a hard time. One day when Mum, Dad and my eldest brother were working up the paddock and I was home with my two sisters and other brother they just got the better of me and I took off.

Our car was parked up the paddock so I got in it and that's where I stayed. When they realised I wasn't around, the hunt was on. I could hear them yelling for me, but I wasn't budging. We had an above ground pool up that summer and they checked in there as well as in the dams to make sure I hadn't drowned.

They searched the stock yards most especially the pig sty because those pigs would eat anything including four year old girls.

I was peeking over the back seat and I saw mum ride past the car a couple of times on the motorbike but she never noticed me. When they finally did look in the car, I pretended I was asleep so I wouldn't get in trouble when they found out I had been hiding from them. Being part of a large family teaches you many things including being sneaky and how to get away with things that you probably shouldn't.

Times when our cousins came to visit were even more fun, because there was double the trouble and more mischief to be had. They lived in the city so coming to the farm was something different for them. We had huge sorghum crops and would have games of hide and seek that would last for hours. We were drafting sheep one weekend while they were there and my eldest cousin decided that he would jump on our old ram and go for a ride. He always liked to show off but this day our old ram got the better of him and sent him flying straight into the fence. It was more than his ego that was bruised that day and he never tried to ride any of the animals again.

We had a picnic down at one of the dams and I have no idea why our parents made us swim there because we knew there were leeches in there but they assured us we would be right. I knew about leeches and what to do but my cousins didn't and I can remember one of them screaming as they ran from the dam absolutely covered in them. I think this may have been a bit of pay back on our parents behalf for all of the mischief we used to get up to.

What I loved most about the farm were the animals, not just the farm animals, there were also the multitudes of butterflies, birds and rabbits. We used to catch wild rabbits and keep them as pets but we also used to go rabbit hunting. I was too little to use the gun but there was always excitement in the chase as you stood up on the back of the ute keeping a look out for them. Our dog also loved the hunt. When he spotted a rabbit he would be off after it and many a time we had to drag him out of the rabbit holes so we could get to the rabbits.

We had owls that would come to sit on our back verandah at night with their beautiful, soulful eyes. They were not tame but they would come to visit us seeking the scraps from the day that we would leave out for them.

After those magical years, reality truly stung when it finally came time to go to school. I had spent most of my time on the farm and about the only contact I had was with my immediate family. When the time came to try to fit into a large group environment it was an extremely difficult adjustment. Before going to school when people came to the farm that I didn't know I would run and hide. There were no pre-schools in those days you were just thrown in the deep end and you had to sink or swim.

I didn't start the same day as the other kids because I had been sick so when I did get there they already knew where they were supposed to be. I ended up in the wrong classroom on my first day and I was more than a little upset especially when the other kids laughed at me. I didn't cry though I managed to keep it together and find the class I was supposed to be in.

By second class I was really starting to enjoy school. Things were set to change again because Mum and Dad decided to move to Forbes. It was exciting because we were going to be living with my Grandmother for a time until we found our own place. Who didn't love going to their Grandma's? I know I did because she would spoil us with chips and lollies which we didn't get at home. Grandma also used to get soft drinks delivered to her house and this was something else we never had, except, of course, when we were at her house.

At the time of the move it was flooding and we all got to sit on the back of our big truck as it drove through the flood waters. We tried to catch fish although that was rather unsuccessful but the fun was had in the trying. We sat on the back of the truck and let our feet dangle in the water as Dad drove us to our new life.

It was a new life that was tinged with many difficulties ahead. Joining into 2nd class in the middle of the year when everyone else was already settled was a challenge that was really hard for this shy girl to handle.

If schooling was difficult in a little town like Grenfell it got even harder in a bigger town with people who already had their friends established and weren't much interested in letting the new girl join their clique. From that move I found it even harder to find my place in the schooling world.

It was with little excitement and much trepidation when it was time to head off to high school. It was a harsh and uncompromising environment where you could easily get lost in the sea of new faces that inundated your life. From the little fish bowl to the big wide ocean and once again it was time to again sink or swim and I barely kept my head above water.

As you go separate ways into different classes from your old friends it was time to make new ones which never came easily to me. I was bullied through primary school and it got worse throughout my high school years. I was one of the first to have braces and there were plenty of taunts from my bullies because of it.

I had a girl become friends with me only so she could make me her scapegoat. I was so naïve thinking this cool chick would want to be friends with a nobody like me. She stole from my sister and said it was me. When I went to stay with her at her sister's place she stole some money off her sister and blamed it on me. I was sent home and never allowed at her place again. There was no way that I could clear myself of doing this and it made me very untrusting of people.

I did make friends and we were a rag tag bunch to say the least. We always hung out in a stairwell at the back of the school to avoid the bullies and their taunts. The only place I ever felt truly comfortable was being in the great outdoors, riding bikes, swimming in the river, camping anything in the wide open spaces that just wasn't school.

The first friend I made in Forbes, Toni, lived across the road from my Grandmother and she was my best friend on and off right throughout my schooling years. When we lived at our farm at "Bedgerabong" Toni would come out and stay sometimes. We were never in the house, we wouldn't even sleep in the house we would put a massive mosquito net over the clothes line and sleep under the stars or we would sleep on the front verandah. We roamed the farm climbing trees, riding bikes, swimming in the river, playing hide and seek in the stables and shearing sheds. We would sneak into the neighbours farm because they had a great forest with some really big old trees that we used to love to climb. On one of our jaunts into the forest we went to walk through a clearing and we came upon a group of wild horses. They weren't happy that we had disturbed them and they started to chase us and we only just managed to get back into the trees to avoid getting trampled. One night a group of us slept on the front verandah and we played truth or dare. I'm not going to mention any names, only to say that it wasn't me, but a couple of people had to do a dare which involved running naked through the Kumbungee reeds down at the dam.

On one particular weekend when Toni came to stay we had had a great weekend but she had to go home on Sunday afternoon. She got changed into her new Bulldog's jersey that her Nan, who she lived with, had given her, but Dad wasn't ready to take her to town, so we went for a walk before she had to go. It was more of an eventful walk than we expected. Our old boar had escaped from his sty and he had us in his sights. I screamed for Toni to run and I jumped over the gate with Toni close behind. I wasn't quick enough to tell her to be careful of the electric fence and she grabbed hold of it. The shock threw her back straight in the mud and animal dung. She didn't want to go home because her Nan could be as 'cranky as that old boar' and she wouldn't be impressed at the state of that jersey. After her Nan did see it Toni was not allowed at the farm for a very long time.

When we moved back into town from our farm near Bedgerabong all my brother's mates would come and stay at our place after they had been to the pub and hung out at our café till it closed in the early hours of the morning. I was a massive tom boy right throughout school and I always ended up being amongst the massive wrestling matches that happened most weekends in our huge rumpus room. I had braces on my teeth and after the third time they got knocked off the orthodontist refused to put them back on. I didn't mind because the buck teeth I had had straightened out enough that people didn't call me Bucky anymore and I hated those awful things anyway.

I was in the midst of one of the famous Forbes wrestling matches when Gary, one of my brother's mates, came up screaming in agony and holding onto his leg and yelling "my foot, my foot". Knowing that it must be something serious we took a look and could see a lump in the fleshy part of the arch of his foot. There must have been a needle in the carpet and it went right into his foot. This occurred on the Friday night of a long weekend and the hospital said they would have to x-ray it first but as it was a long weekend he would have to wait until Tuesday. We thought this was a bit ridiculous because you could clearly see it sticking out.

Another mate whose nickname was Animal, partly because he looked like Animal from The Muppets but mostly because he was the wildest, booziest larrikin to ever venture into Forbes. How this man is still alive is beyond me I have seen him chew the tops of beer bottles crunch it up and swallow it. The night Gary got the needle in his foot, Animal became Dr Black. His medicine just happened to be a bottle of Johnny Walker Scotch. He kept giving Gary shots of it and he ended up extremely drunk but at least he couldn't feel the pain. Gary disappeared on us at one stage and we found him only because he was bleating like a sheep sitting in one of my sisters cupboards. Our family doctor lived down the road from us so the next day Mum took Gary, with a huge hangover, down to see him and all he did was get a scalpel, nick the top and the needle popped out.

I left school in year 10 there was no way I was going to continue on to do Year 11 and 12. I didn't really know what to do after school so I just did what my friends were doing and went to TAFE to do a secretarial course.

My first paying job was when we were still living on the farm digging Bathurst burs in 1000 acre paddocks. After spending two days working every time I closed my eyes all I could see were those darned prickles. I'm glad that job didn't last long. The job that did last a lot longer was my job at the Forbes pool canteen. Every summer from year 7 right through high school and TAFE I worked at the pool canteen for a friend's mum. I was one of the few people that worked for her for the entire time she had the lease because she was a hard person to work for and if you did the wrong thing you were out the door. Her own daughters couldn't work for her because they clashed all the time, but I just kept my head down and did whatever I was told to do. This was a great part time job for me because I heard most of the gossip going around town and I got to perve on the good looking guys who used to hang out at the pool all the time.

There were no full time jobs in Forbes so I headed off to the big smoke, Sydney. Somewhere I never ever really wanted to live but it was an adventure and it was away from Forbes.

My first year in Sydney was the year of the bicentenary and the day after I arrived my sister and I went into Sydney Harbour to watch the tall ships sail in. I couldn't believe how many people could all be in one place. Living in a country town I think the biggest event I ever went to was Carols by Candlelight at the town park at Christmas time. My sister lived in Canberra at the time and she was worried about leaving her little sister in Sydney so she gave me this cute little blue bear, which I called Honey Blue Bear, and that teddy still sits up on my cupboard and watches over me.

My first job in Sydney was with Industrial Relations but they wanted a trainee and I was already fully qualified so they found me another job at the Department of Education. The office was right near Circular Quay. I never got sick of the sight of the harbour as I got off the train to go to work, and I always loved going for walks down to the Quay at lunch time. I worked in the Special Education section and I met some very amazing people while I worked there. Once I got over my shyness and got to know everyone we used to go for lunch on a Friday at the Gallipoli Club which was behind our office block. Friday afternoon never saw much work get done. I saw a different side to some of the people I worked with after these lunches. Everyone was in a much more jovial mood. Some people who I hadn't thought were particularly happy were laughing and skipping as we headed back to our office.

I went on to get a promotion and worked for the Attorney General's Office in the Legislation and Policy Division. The office was on the 20th floor and it had the most amazing views over the Botanic Gardens. It is a pity I never got to admire it much because my job was so busy. I was secretary to the assistant director but also had to do all the typing for the six solicitors in the office. I certainly never had time to get bored on this job there was always interesting work coming across my desk. I typed the legislation which went on to Parliament to change the legal drink-drive limit from .08 to .05 and with the mass amounts of work coming my way my typing speed went well over 100 words per minute.

I was really enjoying life in Sydney but on my first day at The Attorney General's Office I had a fairly scary experience. I had gone for drinks after work to get to know people from the office. I went to Circular Quay station to get the train home. Just before the doors closed this horrible looking guy jumped in. I put my bag on the seat next to me so no one could sit there especially this weirdo. He sat across from me and leaned on the seat in front of him and stared at me. He would get up and walk down to the bottom floor then back to my floor. As he walked back down the aisle he stared at me the whole way.

I was starting to get quite freaked out. Even though it wasn't dark when I got on, it was getting darker as I got closer to my station. When I got off at Homebush I usually walked home because there was no taxi rank there in those days. I kept thinking to myself if everyone gets off at Strathfield, which is the one before Homebush and is much larger, I will get off too. Everyone did get off so I got off. There was a couple there who asked me if I was alright. It was obvious I wasn't and the girl was saying I could just get on the next train but there was no way I was doing that. The guy asked me what I wanted to do. I said I wanted to get a taxi home. I was so frazzled by this stage that I couldn't even think where the taxi rank was. They walked me down there and plenty of people were around so I said thank you to them and I caught a taxi home. I am very grateful to them and that I never saw that weirdo guy again.

Even though I did get homesick sometimes Sydney was an exciting place with so much to see and do. I was hesitant at first but I am really glad that I got to experience Sydney before it got so busy that you can barely move, like it is these days.

Left to right: Craig, Natalie, Michelle, me, Andrew

THE NEXT GENERATION

I got married to Mark when I was only 20. He was the first serious boyfriend I ever had in high school. Mark and I met through my brother. He came to our place one day and he was so fit from being a footballer and BMX rider and with his Greek good looks I couldn't help but be drawn to him.

As he was friends with my brother, we all started hanging out together more often. There was a huge group of us. We would all go bike riding together. I would say I was going to watch Craig race his bike but it was more to see Mark. My grandmother lived on the edge of town with huge paddocks out the back. There was also open land between her place and the train line. We built our own BMX track in one of her paddocks complete with underground bunker made from an old water tank. One night we had a massive bonfire at Grandmas' and everyone was drinking. Mark had an old Ford Cortina Console, and to get it going we had to go and syphon fuel out of someone else's car. Once it was going everyone who was at the bonfire wanted to get in and have a race around the open fields near the train tracks. I was in the car with Mark and a couple of other friends. We were tearing around the paddock at full speed only to come around a corner and one the guys who had had a few too many drinks was lying in the middle of the track. Mark only just managed to swerve in time to miss him.

Mark always seemed to be at our house and when he gave me a friendship ring my mother wasn't happy, she thought it was getting too serious and I was too young. I felt that too because he was always there, and I was so used to being so independent that I felt a little suffocated.

I spoke to my sister who told me to do what felt right for me. Even before I spoke to her I knew that my decision was for us to break up but he was just so devastated. He tried to change my mind but I can be stubborn and I wasn't really mature enough for the relationship to be getting so serious.

After our break up I guess he was hurt and a little angry. We had a combined Year 8 and 11 camp (me being in Year 8 and Mark in Year 11) at Bournda and as we walked through their camp we saw Mark and his friends making rice pudding. When we got close to their camp they started hurling huge spoons full of rice pudding at us. We were far enough away that only a little bit of it hit and we were off to the beach so we just washed it off and made a point of not walking near their camp again.

We went our separate ways and after I finished school and did a secretarial course and moved to Sydney

I got a phone call at my job at the Department of Education. I had no idea who it was. He said "didn't the lady you live with give you the message that I rang on the weekend while you were away?" I told him she hadn't and I still couldn't figure out who it was. He finally told me that it was Mark and we arranged for a meeting. We had arranged to meet for lunch at Rossini Restaurant at Circular Quay. While we were having lunch, a couple of my friends decided they would come down and check out this guy I was meeting. They wouldn't have made very good detectives because we could see them peeking out from behind the pillars.

We got married in 1991 and we were still living in Sydney although we had our wedding at Forbes. When I fell pregnant, we decided that we would move back to the country. We bought a house at Forbes and our first two sons Brendon and Joshua were born there.

Brendon and Josh on Josh's first day of school

CHANGING TIMES

Times were set to change for us because Mark's job on the railways was uncertain, so we made the decision to move to Wollongong before we were forced to move somewhere we didn't want to go.

When we got settled and bought our house in Wollongong we decided that after having two boys we would try for a girl and whatever the outcome that would be our family complete. This was a decision that was not difficult to make, but in the long run very difficult to live with.

We had been trying to conceive for a while but I was very overweight at the time and we weren't sure that I would be able to because of my weight issues. We went out on a scout camp and Mark had bought us tickets to see KISS in Sydney. We left Brendon and Josh at camp and headed off to the concert. Whilst at the concert I started to get stomach cramps. I thought I may have picked some sort of bug up from the camp or that possibly the loud music was making me feel ill. As soon as the camp was over I went to the doctor only to find out that I was pregnant. I wasn't just pregnant, I was about 16 weeks pregnant but due to being overweight, and not having had regular menstrual cycles in years I hadn't realised. The pregnancy, apart from having one episode of back pain, all went just fine up until it was time for the delivery.

Whilst I was in the worst pain of my life, giving birth to a child who I would love and die for, another woman was also giving birth to a child who she couldn't care less for. The midwife had to neglect me for a woman who was giving birth, who happened to be a drug addict. I could hear her running up and down the corridor and screaming at the staff.

When I left my room to head off to the maternity ward the police were there, and I found out that my midwife had been assaulted by this woman and the child had been taken off her. All I ever want for my children is for them to be happy and healthy. I couldn't understand how anyone could take drugs and cause so much damage to a defenceless little life.

Brendon and Josh were easy deliveries compared to Nathan. I have never felt pain like I did the day this child was born. Even though the physical pain left, from the moment I held him in my arms, the emotional pain that he has brought into our world has never left and doesn't get any easier to deal with as he gets older.

Apart from not sleeping very well Nathan was a happy and healthy baby up until 18 months of age.

I don't believe it was just coincidence that he started to have epileptic seizures within weeks of having the MMR injection. I do see medical benefits of getting immunisations for some diseases, but I feel that some of the vaccinations for some children are a trigger for future medical issues.

A couple of weeks after Nathan had his MMR needle, I was walking with him through the lounge room and he looked up at me and in that instant I knew something was wrong. His face went a strange shade of blue and he slumped to the ground. I picked him up and yelled for Mark. As he came, I had to give Nathan CPR because he wasn't breathing. Mark rang the ambulance while I took care of Nathan. The ambulance officers worked on him while I could do nothing but watch on in horror as my boy had a huge seizure. This was the start of six years of seizures.

When Nathan was two, we had to take another ambulance ride but this had nothing to do with having seizures and everything to do with our dog. Nathan was in the back yard playing. I was watching him from the kitchen window as I did the washing up. He was happily running around and then he went over to our dog kennel. The female was in season, so our male was not happy with him intruding. I didn't actually see what happened because Nathan was half inside the kennel but as he pulled his head out of the kennel and looked up at me his face was covered in blood. I knew right away that Bundy had bitten him. I scooped him up checked the wound and knew that it would need stitching.

I went straight to our doctor who was only two blocks over from our house. The doctor saw Nathan straight away, he cleaned up the wound but it was too large for him to deal with in his office. I went back home to try to ring someone to come with me because I knew that it would be difficult trying to find a park and having to deal with Nathan on my own. There was no one around that could help me so I rang an ambulance.

We got to Wollongong Hospital and we had to sit for hours and hours before they could do the surgery on him because he had to be fasted before they could operate. Nathan only got upset once during the day when he saw another kid eating in the room we were in. We sat for almost five hours when they came and said that the theatre was still being used with an emergency and that we would have to wait a bit longer. At the seven hour mark they came back again and asked if we would mind being transferred to Figtree Private Hospital. I was happy to go there but they sent us an ambulance which wasn't able to allow me to sit next to him. When they finally organised the right transport we were off to Figtree. We sat on the gurney as we were being pushed into the hospital and it hit a big bump in the path and Nathan yelled at the top of his lungs "Shit". We really hadn't heard much from him all day and I'm glad there weren't any people around as it was fairly late when we got there but it did give the ambos a good laugh.

I knew by the age of three that Nathan was different from the other kids he used to go to playgroup with at church, he was very hyperactive and he had started the lash out at other kids. I had hoped that when he went to pre-school it would sort itself out but, of course, it didn't. When he did get to preschool the teachers organised for Nathan to be assessed because he was such a handful.

He was four when he was diagnosed with autism. I have heard that so many parents go through a lot of emotions from grief, depression, anger or they will get really upset and cry when they get the diagnosis of autism for their children. I knew nothing about autism when Nathan was diagnosed. When the doctor told me that was what was going on I was just like well how do I fix him. I just assumed that now we had a diagnosis the doctors must know what to do to make his life easier. I could not have been more wrong.

On one occasion Nathan had hit a little girl at preschool. When the father heard about it he told the teachers that if Nathan ever touched his daughter again he would knock his block off. His teacher set him straight and told him he would do no such thing. It is so easy for people to judge. I was horrified that a man could say that he would do something like that to a four year old child. He probably thought he was just a little brat who was allowed to get away with whatever he wanted but that was totally not the case. At the time of this incident they were already organising an aide to be with him while he was at preschool.

He went on to kindergarten at Koonawarra School but as soon as they could get him a place he was sent to the Early Intervention Unit at Mt Warrigal School. The teacher there was such an amazing person and the way she could handle these children was truly inspiring. She worked really hard with Nathan to get him to a stage that he was starting to be able to fit into school and life.

His speech came on really well and his writing skills, while not as good as the other kids, you could read what he was writing. His teachers were always amazed that he could count to 100 before the other kids in his class.

After his stint at early intervention he went back to Kindergarten at Koonawarra. I would sit outside his classroom with the other parents at the end of the day. When Nathan would see me he would put on his biggest smile and hurl himself straight into my arms and give me a huge hug. The other parents used to say "I wish my child would be so excited to see me when I come to pick them up".

Nathan was in the playground one day at school and he started to have a seizure. The school rang me and when I got there the ambulance hadn't yet arrived. When they did finally arrive, after what seemed like ages, they had a hard time getting him to come out of his seizure. They gave him two doses of Intranasal Midazolam which had no effect. When that wasn't having the desired effect, the ambulance officer who was working on him just scooped him up, put him in the ambulance and gave him an injection of the Midazolam. By the time this had been done his seizure had lasted almost half an hour.

All the kids from the infants had been out in the playground when he went into his seizure and the teachers had to get them back to their classrooms. They had all seen what was going on. When I talked to some of the parents afterwards I was told that some of the kids had problems sleeping after seeing it. One of the kids told me that Nathan was bleeding from the eyes. It is quite amazing what kids can imagine, when they see something like this going on.

Nathan still had major speech and development delays and when a new school at Tullimbar, with a dedicated autism class, opened up Nathan was offered a spot. Throughout his time at Tullimbar it was amazing to see the progress that he continued to make. He was happy, content and fitting in really well but he still had a few autistic idiosyncrasies that needed to be sorted out.

Nathan posing with his Pooh Bear

Me, Mark and our three sons (left to right) Josh, Nathan and Brendon

S.T.F.U

WARNING: This chapter contains explicit language. For those of you who don't know what S.T.F.U. stands for it means SHUT THE FUCK UP. Those words will ring in my ears forever for they are the words that Nathan continued to scream over and over again as he lay on the ground in sheer agony after being struck by a car outside the Rivers Store in Bowral. They are also some of the last words he used before he regressed into his autism and stopped talking.

Nathan was 8 years old and the date was 20th January 2010. I will certainly never forget that date because this was the date that was set to turn my world upside down.

I had gone with my Mum to Bowral to see a homeopathic doctor. We were early so we decided to go shopping first. Rivers was the first store we went too. I was looking through some of the clothes and one minute Nathan was standing next to me. The next he was gone. I thought he must have gone to his Nan. When he wasn't with her I went searching for him. By the time I realised he had actually escaped out of the store he had already been hit by a car. I came out of the shop as a man was carrying him off the road. He was apologising for moving him but he wanted to get him to safety. He laid him gently down on the footpath and as I was about to ask someone to call an ambulance I heard the wail of the sirens.

As Nathan lay on the ground screaming and the ambulance officers were looking after him, I looked up at my Mum and tears were brimming in her eyes. I couldn't look back at her again because I didn't want to end up being an emotional wreck. I just needed to focus on my boy and getting him the help he needed.

As he lay on the ground he continued to scream "Shut the fuck up car" over and over. The ambos were not fazed by his screaming and told me not to worry about it as they had heard much worse. It was still rather embarrassing as all these people were gathering around and my child is screaming at the top of his lungs at the car that hit him.

Before I could get in the ambulance to go to the hospital I had to make sure that Mum was alright. A police officer had arrived, and he said he would make sure Mum got over to the hospital to be with us after she had been to see the doctor we were supposed to see to let him know about the accident.

Instead of seeing just one doctor, which was our intent in going to Bowral, that day we saw many doctors and health professionals. When we got to the hospital they had to cut off his brand new clothes he had just got for Christmas because they didn't want to move him too much as they didn't know what sort of injuries he may have sustained. Nathan had gone to sleep on our way to the hospital and no one could get him to wake up. There was a lot of concern that he was so sound asleep and he was taken off to get a whole load of scans. The doctors were worried that he may have hit his head on the ground when the car had hit him.

While he was getting his scans done there was one thing I had to do which I was dreading. I had to ring his Dad. This was a very hard thing to do because we had been separated at the time. We had been separated since 2008. I moved out with Nathan, Brendon and Josh, who were in high school at the time, stayed with Mark. It broke my heart to break my family up but I left because I could no longer handle all the arguments and being blamed every time something went wrong. I moved into a house close to Brendon and Josh so they could come and see me whenever they wanted to.

There was so much guilt in me at the time for allowing Nathan to get hurt that made that phone call very difficult to make. I was so worried that he would blame me and we would get into another fight because of it but I'm glad to say that didn't happen. There was just concern for Nathan. He and Josh made it to Bowral in record time. I'm not saying they were speeding but Josh did say they got airborne as they drove over the train tracks outside Bowral.

I went back to waiting for Nathan to return from his scans with a whole load of trepidation weighing me down. The doctors concern that he wouldn't wake was worrying me and as they wheeled him back to me he looked so peaceful. They said there was no brain injury and everything seemed to be fine. The only conclusion they could come to was that he was sleeping due to the trauma of the accident.

When he did wake up he was taken to a ward for observation. When he came too there was great relief but as he got up to go to the toilet he kept screaming. We almost had to carry him to the toilet because he couldn't stand on his right leg. Every time he tried to put weight on it he would scream and cry.

This time he was wheeled up to X-ray and they found that he had actually fractured his hip bone. There was nothing they could do for this injury and they said it would heal on its own but it would be quite painful for a while. It was broken in a spot that would cause no arthritis as he gets older. We had to stay in the hospital for two nights to be sure that he was alright.

On Australia Day which was six days after his accident we had been swimming. As I was drying Nathan off and getting him dressed he kept getting upset every time I touched his wrist. He would wince and I could tell there was something wrong with it. I rang Mark and told him I was worried that there was something wrong. He told me he would take him to the hospital. I said it would be better to wait until the next day because it was Australia Day and Wollongong Hospital would be bedlam. We were going back to Bowral the next day so I said we would just go and see the doctors who treated him there. I am so glad we did because they were great. Within four hours we had seen the doctors been x-rayed, found out the arm was broken, had his cast put on and we were on our way home again. I have spent a lot of time in Wollongong Hospital and I knew that it would have been a much longer day.

Nathan's hip healed up surprisingly fast and within a couple of weeks he was walking without a limp. The cast was supposed to be on his arm for four weeks but during the third week he shoved a pen in it with the lid still on. The pen came out but the lid didn't. I was concerned that we couldn't get it out and it was obviously irritating him a lot. It was the weekend so I decided that I would cut it off myself. I very, very carefully cut it off and inside was all sorts of things - leaves, twigs and, of course, the pen lid.

Even though his injuries healed up quickly with no long term physical side effects, the emotional side effects of the accident have never left him and have changed his world forever.

Not only has Nathans accident changed his world, it has left me with a huge amount of guilt and pain for allowing him to get hurt. It doesn't matter how many times people say to me you can't blame yourself for what happened, I still do.

2010 - THE YEAR THAT WAS

2010 - the year that was the worst year and the year that was the best in so many ways.

It was the worst year because this was the year that Nathan got hit by the car. This accident was a huge turning point in our lives and as I said earlier Mark and I had been separated at the time. The accident made us take a step back and look at our lives and in so doing we realised that we could not deal with all of Nathan's issues on our own. We were only two days from our divorce being finalised and come what may we went to the court house and cancelled the proceeding and I moved back home.

Coming home was such a happy time in our life and it felt so right to be back in our house with my boys all back together again. Apart from the issues we had with Nathan things were going well until November when Mark went on a social golf trip with his work mates down to Batemans Bay. I received a phone call from Mark at 3 am on Sunday morning. As soon as I heard his voice I knew something was wrong. He asked me if I could go and pick him up because he had been beaten up. I dragged Nathan out of bed and off we drove the almost three hours to pick him up.

The man who did this was supposed to be a friend but he was extremely drunk at the time. He had been drinking beer while they played golf during the day. We were told when they were at the pub he had been drinking Jager Bombs as well as Vodka and Red Bull. Mark hadn't gone to the pub with them but he heard some of them come back to the hotel. He was standing at his hotel door talking to one of his mates when another one came over and he wanted Marks room because he had bought a female back and didn't have his room key. Mark told him to go away and as he turned to shut the door he was king hit in the side of the head and was continued to be beaten until he was black and blue. Mark is only 5'5" and this guy was well over 6 feet tall.

When I got there Mark had already been to the hospital and had stitches in his ear and above his eyebrow. He had a black eye and bruises on his chest. Mark hadn't talked to the police and after much discussion I finally convinced him that he needed to press charges. We went to the Dapto Police Station when we got back to set the wheels in motion.

On the Tuesday after the assault I went to TAFE and about 12pm I started to feel unwell so I decided to go home. When I got home I went up to check on Mark only to find him disoriented and he kept saying

"There is blood running down my head". I convinced him there wasn't but I knew something was terribly wrong. I took him straight to our doctor and he sent him over to get a head scan. We went back to the doctors and he told us that Mark had a fractured skull and that was what the feeling was that Mark was having. It was from the inside of his head that gave him the feeling that blood was running down his head. Due to his injuries had to take six weeks off work.

The case went to court and it had to be held at Batemans Bay because that is where the assault happened. We attended the first court case because Mark had to testify and the judge told us we didn't have to attend the next one if we didn't want to, but we wanted to be there to hear the outcome. It wasn't what we were expecting. The judge had said that he didn't believe the other guys story because of the amount of injuries that Mark had sustained but he couldn't give a guilty verdict because he couldn't ascertain who had started the fight.

Sadly that meant that he gotten away with it but he was not allowed to work at the same station as Mark from then on and was sent to Campbelltown. Not long after he assaulted Mark he got into an altercation with transit officers which was captured on CCTV footage and because of this he lost his job. It seems that karma does have a way of catching up with some people.

Up until 2010 the church was a huge part of my life. When I first started attending I helped out with the women's group and I helped start up and run the new girls group that was held on a Thursday night. After Nathan had his accident one person from the church dropped in to give me a meal. She stayed for about two minutes and I never saw another person.

I always thought a church community is supposed to be a loving, supportive one who helped people who are suffering. Not only was Nathan suffering but so was I and with the lack of support I received from them I started to feel that all I had done over the years was for nothing and that we were unimportant. I have always struggled with my faith and at this point it all but disappeared and I cannot now bring myself to step foot into that church.

In December 2010 I was excited because I managed to get myself a job. The main reason I wanted to get work was so I could try to get help for Nathan. I hadn't worked for a few years so it was good to be getting paid again. I became a mobile nurseryperson looking after plants in office buildings.

2010 had some massive highs and lows and I wish I could go back and change many things that happened but I am glad that year is over and done with and I hope I never have another one like that.

My Year In Colour

Blue zircon skies draw us into the new year
Supposed to be a good one but chaos reigns from the onset
Dark obsidian clouds threaten our very existence
Mocha and smoky topaz whirlpools swirl around
Ruby, dark coral and siam hurt the eyes
Crystalised white opal teardrops fall down as injuries abound

Teetering on the edge looking down into the abyss
An amber ray of light shines down
A rainbow appears
Love long lost has once again been found
Wraps you in its warm rose velvet glow

Lilac, sweet lavender and amethyst welcome you in
Moving on, moving home warms the heart
Life moves on with a melodious copper-tone pace
Painting and sculpting new but familiar tones
Rich as gold we follow this every changing path

Emerald green hills fade quickly
Deep, dark sepia storms roll in
The hot chilli red of an angry night takes over
In the glowing embers is left the bitterness
Hatred subsides, healing begins

The art of life is constant and all -consuming
Colours swirl, flash and flare as time moves swiftly
Don't allow the dark depths to devour you
Dream sweetly and allow the glorious, gentle hues to flow
And always behold the beauty that surrounds you

By Sonia Facey

In 2010 I was doing a Visual Arts course and one of the classes was Cultural Productions which included written art. At the end of the year our teacher got us to write poem entitled "My Year in Colour" and this was the poem I wrote.

SILENCE ISN'T ALWAYS GOLDEN

The dramas of 2010 kept coming because when Nathan went back to school and he wasn't speaking, the teachers were unsure how to help him. They were also concerned for Nathan's safety because the school is out in the open and it couldn't be fully fenced and Nathan kept attempting to run away. A lot of discussion occurred about how to help Nathan and it was decided that the following year he would once again move schools. We transferred him to Para Meadows School. The school is fully fenced and it caters specifically to children with disabilities.

I had my reservations about moving him because I still wanted him to be around children who were speaking and most of the kids at the new school didn't speak at all. In the end I felt I had no choice and it has been a good move because there are so many teachers with a lot of experience in dealing with difficult children and Nathan has certainly become a very difficult child.

There is grief in loss and I have had some times of immense grief at the loss of Nathan's ability to speak. I know there are children who have never ever said a word but in Nathan's case he was talking quite well and when he stopped those feelings of grief at the loss of his voice sweep over at times. When he is having a meltdown I just wish he would use his words again so he could tell me what is wrong so we can help him.

He will say some words now but only when he is highly motivated. When he hears the dominos ads on the radio he will say pizza and if he is hungry he will say sometimes ask for a burger or chips. He just refuses to use any of the skills that he used to have.

He understands what we say very well because I can ask him to do things and he will do it. It may take him longer than your average child to take the information in and then do what I ask him but it eventually sinks in and he gets it done unless he's in one of his moods then nothing gets done.

None of the doctors we have been to have been able to tell us why he chooses to be mute, except that it could be trauma from the accident, when it would be so much easier for him to express in words what he needs and wants.

When I go through the videos I have of him from when he was speaking I have to laugh because he was such a cheeky little bugger. I was bathing him one morning before school and all he wanted to do was lie in the bath. I needed to get him ready for school but he refused to get out. I told him to pull the plug out and all he would say was no. I reached for the plug and he said "Let go of that pug". He couldn't pronounce the "L" properly. I reached for the plug again and he said "just go away, go to bed, just go away". I reached again for the plug and he yelled at me and told me to piss off and shut the fuck up. I told him I would wash his mouth out with soap (not that I would it was just a threat) and he said "no soap, throw it down the drain, chuck it down the drain, throw it down the drain".

In another of the videos I have, Brendon had come in when Nathan was eating a hamburger and he had chips as well. When Brendon went to eat some of his chips he started screaming at the top of lungs "PISS OFF BRENDON" and he would do it every time Brendon went to take a chip. He had his burger in one hand and picked up the paper that it had been in and threw it at Brendon. Lettuce went everywhere. He certainly didn't want Brendon eating his chips and he was vocalising that very well.

Looking back through that footage also makes me a little sad because of how much of our cheeky little boy we lost when he got hit by that car.

Recently Nathan got cranky with Brendon and he blurted out "Shut the Fuck up Brendon". As horrified as most people would be to hear their child swear this way I was delighted. It showed me that those skills are still there but we just can't seem to find a way to help him get them back again.

One day while I was cooking dinner and Brendon was playing with Nathan chasing him around the house. Nathan was squealing and he ran into the kitchen and yelled out "MUM". I was so amazed I had to stop what I was doing and give him a big hug. I almost shed a tear because I hadn't heard him call me mum in such a long time. He ran off again as Brendon chased him and I continued on cooking with a new enthusiasm and hope that even though the progress is extremely slow Nathan will be able to have a conversation with me again one day.

SEEK & DESTROY

Post the trauma of the injuries Nathan suffered in his escape from the Rivers Store life has tumbled down into one meltdown after another. We have gone from having a child who was learning to cope with his world, that was so much different from the one that we understand, to having a child who could no longer cope with the stimuli that this world inflicts on him.

When Nathan gets overloaded he goes into meltdown mode and the first thing that happens is he targets something that he can take his frustration out on. He is like a targeting missile seeking out his enemy and hitting just the right point to do as much damage as possible whether it be one of us, himself or whatever he can get his hands on. Most of the times it is the walls and if you come to our house and have a look at all my artworks on the wall you may think they aren't too bad but if you take a look behind them you will find that most of them have been strategically placed over yet another hole in the wall.

When he was about three there was one thing that he did destroy, but it was not intentional, was the chandelier which hangs in our stair well. He was leaning over the bannister and playing with it and spinning it around. At the time Mark's computer desk was in the space at the bottom of the stair well. He just happened to look up as Nathan leant over a little too far and came crashing through the light. Mark only just managed to grab him and stop him falling flat on his back on the wooden floor. His feet slapped the floor so hard the sound was horrendous. Luckily he didn't do any damage to them. The only damage was to the light he broke a couple of the glasses and it has never hung straight since then.

In our lounge room we started plastering up the holes he created but every time we did, he would target that spot again so we decided that we would use wooden floor boards to make feature walls over the holes. There is no way he is going to go through the walls now. He has given it a try, however, and when he couldn't get the satisfaction of going through those walls he went to find somewhere else he could put holes.

We had to replace his bedroom door with a solid wooden one because when we would take him to his room he would kick and punch the coir door that was on there until bit by bit, he managed to totally destroy it. We got the new door put on and he started to kick the door and the hinges weren't as solid as they could have been. He managed to knock it off its hinges completely when he walked into his room and shoved it back against the wall. I had to go and buy more hinges to make it more solid. It now has five hinges on it instead of just three so hopefully it is now solid enough for him not to knock it off again.

From an early age he has shredded things like catalogues, newspapers and leaves. He was in the back yard and I had small camellia tree growing and when I wasn't watching he pulled every leaf off it. I thought he had killed it but the next season it came back. Once again when I wasn't looking he pulled all the leaves off it and this time it didn't come back. I wasn't impressed because it was really pretty and I haven't seen one like it again.

I very rarely take Nathan anywhere near shops on my own because I can't control him if he goes into a meltdown. Even when someone comes with me, we have to be watching him like a hawk and we have to be right next to him all the time. I took him into a mall once, and because he was overwhelmed from all the stimuli that was bombarding him, he started to get agitated. Brendon was with me and as we were leaving we walked past the seafood shop Nathan hit one of the glass panels but it didn't break, thankfully. The owner yelled at me to take my child home. Brendon took him to the car and I tried to apologise and tell him that he had autism and that he didn't mean it. He just said to me "take your little prick home". I used to buy my fish and chicken from there all the time, but I will never buy another thing from that shop.

Another time when I took him to the chiropractor he went into her office calmly and allowed her to do some cranial massage and adjust his back, without any dramas. It wasn't until we went to walk out into the car park that I could see a change in him and I tried to get him to the car but he took off and ran straight at the colourbond fence. He damaged two panels but we were very lucky he didn't go through them. I talked to the owner and she said don't worry her husband could straighten them out as they were only slightly bent.

I have to be careful leaving pens and paperwork sitting around because Nathan will draw on anything including himself. Our bathtub has become multi-coloured because Nathan will draw all over himself, and when I give him a bath the ink transfers to the tub. He will sit and draw, mostly it is just scribble, for ages. When his frustration takes over, he will snap whatever he is drawing with in half. I couldn't say how many pens and pencils I have had to throw in the bin.

There have been so many things that Nathan has destroyed. Just a few of the things that have happened in the last year, apart from the continual destruction of the walls, including two windows in his room, three Ipads and my television.

I was getting Nathan ready for school one morning and he was being really good but I heard him hit something and I didn't take much notice because he didn't do it again. I got him on the bus and had to go out for the day. When I got home I went to turn my laptop on only to find that it wouldn't come on as the screen was smashed. It was only then that I realised that it was my laptop that Nathan had hit that morning. I had a moment where I thought he had destroyed it altogether. We were able to hook it up a computer screen and it still worked. I was really annoyed, more so with myself, for leaving it on the lounge because I usually put it away but this day I just forgot. To say I was relieved that it was working would be an understatement because I had just done a huge on edit on this book and hadn't backed it up onto a hard drive yet.

Josh, who is really good at fixing things, bought me a new screen and put it in for me. He did such a good job that it is working just as good as it was before.

My friend messaged me on Facebook and jokingly said "What did the laptop do to him?". I replied "it must have looked at him the wrong way". Her reply back to me was "at least you have a sense of humour". All you can do sometimes is to find a way to have a laugh at the situation or you would go crazy.

At one stage we had to take everything hard out of his room because when he would go into meltdown mode he would try to either pick things up and throw them or he would overturn them. He ended up having only a mattress on the floor and his clothing in the cupboard.

He has even attacked his curtains and in the process broken a number of curtain rods. After the first time he started pulling on the curtains I thought it might be better to put in curtain wire but the first meltdown he had after I put that up he just absolutely destroyed the wire. I had to change tack and get thick round hooks which I put in the middle with just normal open cup hooks on the ends. This seemed to work until he had a really huge meltdown one day and pulled so hard that he just totally bend the end cup hook. We then had to put a solid hook on the end as well and up until now that has worked.

The worst thing to watch is when he does damage to himself. Last year Nathan kept holding his right arm as if it was sore. After a few days I realised that it was really quite swollen. We have no idea when or how he did it but when I took him to the doctor we found out that he had actually broken it. The same day we found this out we also found out that he had contracted scabies. I had to deal with the scabies before he could get his cast put on.

Trying to get a cast on a normal child can be quite difficult but when you have a teenage autistic child it is almost impossible. Brendon and I had to hold him while the physiotherapist had to work extremely hard to get the cast on. He only had it on for one day when we had to go back and get more fibro put on it because he had started to pull on the ends of it, and if we didn't, he would have destroyed it. After we got this on we had to get super glue because he was still trying to pull on it. Almost every day he had it on I had to put more super glue where he had been trying to rip bits of it off.

It was really starting to irritate him and after the third week it was really starting to smell bad, like rotten flesh, and he was really upset with it. Brendon and Josh were with me one weekend and we decided that we would cut it off. Brendon got this tool that looked somewhere between a pair of pliers and scissors. I held onto Nathan while he cut through the cast. It was very tough because of all of the super glue that we had used on it. When we got to the really thick part around his thumb there was no way we were going to cut through it with the tool we had. Josh put a small cutting tool on the air compressor and very carefully and slowly cut through the cast. When we got it off there was a whole heap of leaf matter and sticks in the cast. His skin was so red and irritated it looked like it had been burned. We had to get antibiotic cream to get his skin cleared up.

I would never have thought that one child could cause so much destruction not only to our house but to himself.

This occurred one night when we had a party. We had to put him in his room. He went to town on the wall.

We had to use 12mm MDF board to cover it up.

These are some of the holes in our lounge room that we have had to cover up

This is one of our cover up feature walls

Newspaper fight on Christmas Eve with all the newspaper Nathan had ripped up

SCARRED

On our journey in this life we all incur some sort of physical and emotional scarring and there are many different ways to cope with these scars. For me the hardest scars to recover from have been the emotional scars inflicted right from my youngest years in school, to coping with a father with bi-polar disorder, a divorce and now living with a loving, cuddly but on the flip side a violent, destructive and uncontrollable child with autism.

The emotional scars are like the sands on the beach. People don't see them most of the time because they are hidden by the ocean. Then crash, one huge wave, or even a tiny one can expose all that is hidden beneath.

After a particularly stressful and painful morning with Nathan I had to attend an information workshop on the new National Disability Insurance Scheme. We were having a discussion on different aspects of the new scheme. The topic of families having to give up their children because they can no longer look after them came up, then, crash, there came this wave of emotion and all those sands that were covered by the ocean were uncovered. I was, all of a sudden, in tears in front of all these people who I had never met before. I was rather embarrassed, but knowing these people all deal with particularly difficult situations of their own made it just a little easier to deal with.

The physical scars are the ones that are a little harder to hide. They are an ever present and a constant reminder that this life is an extremely difficult place to be.

Nathan has incurred more scars, in his short life, than most people incur in their lifetime. His first scars were the two he received from our dog. One is in his left eyebrow and the other is in his hairline. You can only see these ones if you know they are there as he was so little when he received these.

The doctor started him on a new medication in 2012 and while on this one he started head-butting walls. He hasn't only head-butted the plaster walls in our house but he has head-butted brick walls when he has been in a state of utter frustration. He has a permanent lump on his forehead now.

During his meltdowns he just doesn't seem to feel pain. He will punch himself in the legs and elbow walls and he will also punch himself in the face over and over until he is covered in bruises. I have seen my boy run head first at a wall and continue to bang his head on the wall over and over. During one of these meltdowns he fell and hit his head on the window sill and cut his head open. When he has gotten in this state it has taken two, and sometimes three of us, to hold him down to stop him hurting himself.

He has a scar on his left upper thigh from a time when I caught him attempting to escape from our yard. He was up on the fence and when I busted him and told him to get down he rushed and caught his leg on one of the posts. It would have healed up really well but he kept picking at it, causing it to be much larger than it would have been if he had left it alone.

His most evident scars are the ones on his hands from biting himself during his meltdowns. When he does bite his hands they take a very long time to heal because as soon as they start to heal up he pulls the scab off and makes them bleed again.

His most recent scar occurred on Anzac Day night this year. He was having a bath and I left the bathroom to go and get a towel, I wasn't gone very long and in the instant I was gone he flipped out and put his elbow through the wall. The tiles smashed and because they were so sharp he cut his arm to pieces. It was so scary because there was so much blood in the bathtub.

I couldn't drive him to hospital because I had had a few drinks, so it had to be an ambulance ride again. Brendon came with me to help out with Nathan. We were taken to a quiet room to wait until he had fasted long enough, so they could give him the gas to do work on his arm.

The first attempt to get the gas on him to knock him out was very unsuccessful because we just couldn't hold him still enough to get the mask on him. The nurse went in search of someone who was available to come back and help out. He came back with two big burly security guards. One of them had to hold his legs and the other had to lay across his body to keep him still. I was lying across his chest with my ear right near his mouth. They had to give him a needle and when they stuck the needle in he let out a massive scream. It was so loud I thought he was going to deafen me. Brendon had hold of his head to keep it still so the nurse could keep the gas mask on him.

The gas causes Nathan to get giggly, so when it took effect we all still had to hold him as the doctor knelt on the floor and went to work on the wound. The doctor was using super glue to fix his wound and there was blood pouring out of his arm but Nathan was still giggling. I asked the staff if I could take the gas home it would certainly make my life easier if he were giggling, rather than destroying himself and the house.

When the doctor was finished she put a light weight cast over the wound to stop him picking at it. We went home about one on a Sunday morning, and he was fine with the cast until the early hours of Monday morning. I went to get him out of bed and there was blood and bits of plaster cast everywhere and he was picking at the wound.

We had to make another trip back to the hospital to get it stitched up this time and have a full fibreglass cast put on. The cast was a huge source of frustration for Nathan, so much so that he started hitting people with it. Mum was visiting, and he hit her a couple of times with it. It must have been so uncomfortable for him and that was his only way of telling us that he was having a hard time coping with it.

He kept trying to pull the cast apart and I tried everything to get him to leave it alone. I made a lycra sock which I cable tied over the cast but he managed to rip that to shreds after about three days.

He was supposed to have the cast on for at least two weeks but after the first week it smelled like something had crawled inside the cast and died. I decided to take him back to hospital because I was concerned his arm had become infected. I was already exhausted before we went in to the hospital because during the day, while Nathan had been at school, I went to see my sister who was in hospital at Goulburn.

Once again we had to wait for him to be fasted so they could knock him out to cut the cast off. One of the nurses was saying she didn't think we were going to like what was going to be under that cast when it came off from the smell of it. She was thinking that it was going to be pretty badly infected too. They came in with the saw and cut it off and to everyone's surprise it wasn't infected. Nathan had been elbowing walls with the cast which caused the wound to bleed. The smell was from the blood and other fluids that were in the cast. They took the stitches out and he was given antibiotics to take to make sure it didn't get infected. Another nurse came and put heaps of dressings and bandages over the wound and we finally got home again around midnight. I slept in Nathans room with him to make sure he didn't pull at the dressings. I sent him to school with ski gloves cable tied on his hands but by 12.30 the school rang me to say that he had shredded the gloves with his teeth.

Nathan, like a lot of other kids with autism, don't like things stuck on their skin. He won't ever leave a band aid on for more than a few minutes, so all I could think of to do so the wound was protected was to put a long sleeve shirt on him with a sanitary pad stuck on the inside of the sleeve.

I hope there aren't too many more scars for my boy in the future for his sake and because those trips to the hospital are getting harder and harder to cope with, as he gets bigger.

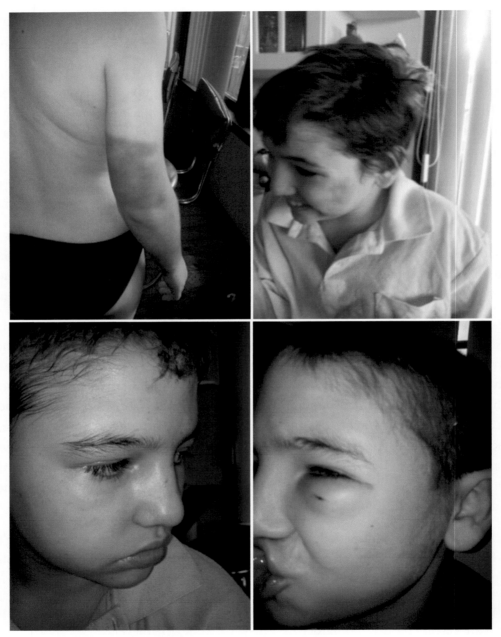

Just a few of the injuries Nathan has inflicted on himself.

Here Nathan is with the cast he had to have on to try to stop him ripping his stitches out

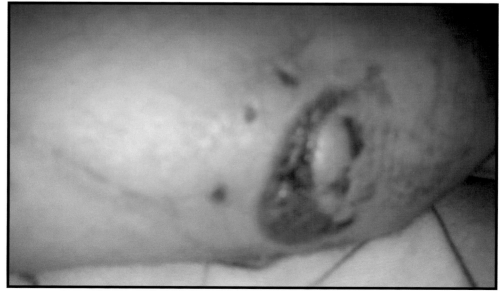

This is what the wound looked like after the cast came off

SOME HEFTY FIGHTS

Fighting seems to be a way of life for me. Not that I get into any sort of physical fights, that is not me. I would rather talk my way out of any type of difficult situation. My fighting is of the emotional kind.

Right from an early age I have struggled to fit in this world. This started right from the time I left my magical world of our farm and was thrust into the school world. Right through school I had to fight off the stigma of having a mentally ill father. Along with having an ill father came the fact that we were poor and this, growing up, was harder to deal with at school than having a sick dad. I don't think most of the kids knew how ill my dad really was but it was evident we were poor because we never had money to buy food at the canteen. One of the bullies called me a scab because my friends used to always be sharing their snacks with me. I never got to do the extra curricula activities, and the worst was having to wear hand me downs from my sisters. Winter came around and all I had to wear to school were these old out-dated nylon trousers. I think this was when I developed a tolerance to the cold because the bullies used to give me a hard over them and I chose to wear my summer uniform instead no matter the weather.

Another fight that I have had to deal with is my weight. Through my early adult years I have always struggled to keep my weight under control but when the Brendon and Josh came along I lost that battle and ended up becoming obese. I was still obese after Nathan was born and when he was about two, I decided that I had to do something about it. At my heaviest I was 104 kilos and this was definitely not where I wanted to be. I started reading and trying to decide the best way to deal with it. I think I read every book in the library on diets before I decided on taking the Atkins approach. I had tried many things along the dieting journey and for me this was the one that worked the best. On this diet I managed to lose 40 kilos to get to a weight that I was extremely happy with.

In the last year with the problems I had with work and Nathan I allowed myself to put back on 10 of those kilos. Once again I have to fight to get back to where I am at my fittest and healthiest.

I have another fight I am fighting at this current time and that is to save Nathan's respite centre which the government wants to abandon. I was sitting in my car one day when a news announcement came on the radio saying that the centre was set to close. As soon as I could I went to the centre to find out what was going on. I was disgusted that the parents and carers were not informed that this was going to happen.

When I found out about it I knew I had to do something so I started a petition. I am attempting to get it to 10,000 signatures so that it can go to parliament to be debated.

The way the government was trying to close this centre was utterly despicable. I had a respite planner come to my house and I was told that if I didn't sign over to a non-government organisation I may not get funding. Then I found out that they were not signing up any more clients to come into the centre. By scaring parents into signing over to a non-government organisation and not letting any new kids in, they would then have been able to say that the centre wasn't functional so that would be there way to close it. I knew I had to find a way to expose what was happening so I went to my local member, Anna Watson. She went to parliament with a list of questions to ascertain what was going to happen with the centre. She also contacted the Minister for Family and Community Services and she did a press release about what was happening. By highlighting the issue she was able to get a guarantee that the centre would be open until July 2016.

I have written to many different ministers about this situation and when I got no responses that made any sense I decided to write a letter to our premier - Mike Baird but I got no response from him only a letter from his office palming me off to yet another minister. This is the letter which I sent to him.

Dear Mr Baird

I WONDER HOW YOU WOULD FEEL????

I wonder how you would feel if you were scared of your 12 year old child. If you lived each day fearing that this child was going to give you a black eye, a broken jaw or any number of other injuries.

I wonder how you would feel having to watch your child punch themselves in the face so hard you thought they would knock their own teeth out or biting their own arms so hard they rip out chunks of skin. As a parent you have no idea what that is like to watch.

I wonder how you would feel having to know the layout of your local hardware store back to front because your child does new damage to your house almost every day. Today it could be a smashed window, tomorrow it could be more holes in the walls.

I wonder how you would feel having to learn to use every power tool in the shed because you can't afford to pay a tradie to come and continually fix the damage to the house.

I wonder how you would feel if your child couldn't participate in any of the extra-curricular activities that average children enjoy every day like sports, scouting, learning to play a musical instrument. Even just a walk in the park can become a nightmare.

I wonder how you would feel having to become a jailer for your child because you don't want them to escape from your house and have to go searching the neighbourhood looking for them and hoping and praying they haven't been hit by a car or taken by a paedophile.

I wonder how you would feel not being able to take family holidays. Not being able to see the delight on your child's as they ride the roller coaster or come splashing down a water slide.

I wonder how you would feel as you become more and more reclusive because you can't take your child out in public for fear of them hitting someone or smashing up a shop.

I wonder how you would feel never sleeping properly because of the stress this child causes to your life but still having to get up and go to work even though all you want to do once you have got your child on the bus to school is crawl back in your warm, comfortable bed and fall into so deep a sleep that the nightmare you live each day will cease to haunt your dreams.

I'm not going to say that any of this is unfair it is just our life. Our son, Nathan, has autism and this is what we live each and every day.

What is unfair is the government shutting down the respite centre he attends a few days each month so the rest of the family can get a little rest. I am petitioning the government not to do this to all the families in the Illawarra who use this much needed facility.

I appreciate the fact that you came to the Illawarra recently to open up a new and exciting business but I feel while you were here you could have taken some time to look at some of the real issues facing the Illawarra. One of them being the closure of the Dapto Respite Centre. Maybe you could have visited the centre and met the wonderful, amazing staff who take such good care of the many children affected with disabilities. It is not only the families affected by this but the staff as well because their future is unclear also.

I have been trying to get answers as to what is going to happen to the centre. Every person I contact tells me something different. One minister told me it is under review, another sent me a letter filled with so much political ramble that in the end I was more confused than ever. I have been told by an ADHC worker that we may not even get any respite in the Illawarra.

As a loving family man I am hoping that you will take into consideration not only my families needs but the needs of all the families in the Illawarra who use the Dapto Respite Centre. I look forward to hearing from you in relation to this matter.

Yours sincerely

Sonia Facey

I waited and waited for a response and when I get a letter in the mail from the Premiers office I thought I was going to get some answers. I was horrified to find that it was just a letter from his staff saying that they had passed my concerns on to another minister. To this day I cannot understand how any person could not respond to a letter like this.

I have had so many people tell me they think I am doing a really good thing by running with this petition, but I just say I am doing what I can to try to help my family and many other families in the Illawarra. It is just something that I feel any parent in my position should do. I know that it is extremely unlikely that I will win the fight to save Nathan's centre but I can't sit back and not try.

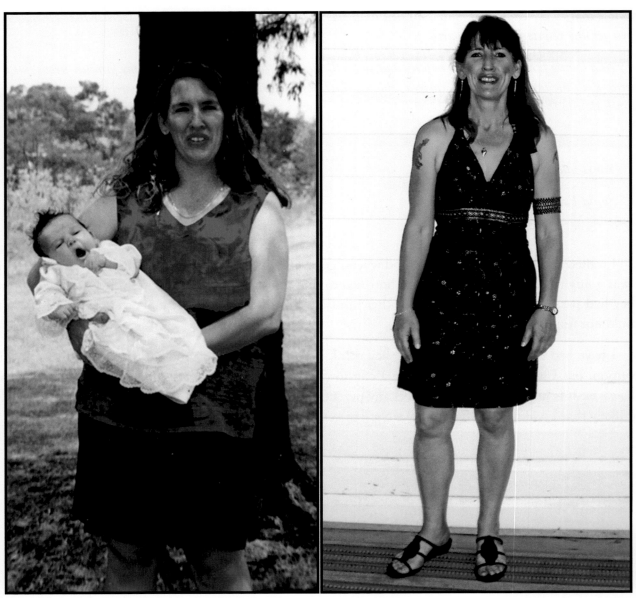

Before and after on my weight loss journey

THE NUTELLA BANDIT

Children with autism often like to go wandering and Nathan is certainly one of those children. When he was younger he used to climb out of our yard and just go wandering around our street.

There have been many times he has done more than just go wandering he has actually run away. One Monday afternoon during the school holidays when Nathan was still attending Tullimbar School he must have gotten bored and decided he wanted to go back to school. We started searching for him but it was starting to get dark so I had to contact the police. I had people out searching everywhere for him. In the end the police arrived at our house with Nathan in toe. A very concerned lady had seen him wandering, with no shoes on, and rang the police. He was out the back of Dapto almost at the freeway that would have taken him to his school. I have always been astounded by his sense of direction.

On the Friday of that same week we went to Yass to visit my sister. She lived about five kilometres out of town and we were watching him on the trampoline as we ate our dinner. I went inside to put my plate in the dishwasher and when I came back out he was gone, again with no shoes.

I have no idea how he could have gotten away so fast. It was like he was gone in the blink of an eye. It was getting dark once again so we had to call the police. They were calm and easy going which was very different to the police in Wollongong who made me answer a million questions and made me feel like a bad mother. We were getting panicked though because there was so much open space and dams that he could have fallen into and he didn't know the area. The police checked all around the paddock and they reckoned that as it was getting dark he would head to the lights of the town.

My sister had her neighbours out helping to look for him. Their son, who was on his P's, came back to the house with Nathan in his car. The police were right because he found him on the outskirts of Yass and he just hopped into his car. It is very scary that he will just get into a car with a total stranger.

As he has gotten older, so has his hunger. Instead of just going wandering, he has started to go in search of food. The first time he went off in search of food was to our favourite burger shop. It is about four kilometres from our home. It is fairly easy to get there as you only have to turn a few corners but there are a couple of challenges along the way. That first challenge is it is a long way, once again barefoot, and the other is getting across one of the busiest roads in Dapto.

We were out searching all over the place for him and we couldn't find him anywhere in our neighbourhood. We put the call out on Facebook and had everyone on the lookout for him. Brendon and Josh were on their bikes. Brendon thought he saw Nathan in a car so he rang me and I headed in that direction. Fearing that he had been picked up by a paedophile I was getting frantic. As I headed in the direction of where Brendon thought he had seen him my phone rang. Mark had received a call from his school to say one of the teachers had seen him heading down Kanahooka Road near the Dandaloo Shops. I immediately knew where he was heading. He had headed off to the café to get a burger. At that point in time the café owners didn't really know us but they certainly do now. He was determined to get behind their counter and at the food. They gave him a few chips which kept him content until we got there.

The relief of knowing that he was now safe, and not in the hands of a paedophile, did not outweigh the fact that he had run away from home. I can guarantee you that he didn't get a burger that day, instead he was taken straight home and put in his room. I was most certainly not going to reward him by letting him get away with running away from home and trying to scare the life out of us.

Since that day he has never taken off to the burger shop again. He has since found a shop much closer to home. Our local IGA which is only about a 10 minute walk or a 2 minute run for Nathan when he is on the hunt for food.

One day when he had run away we were all out looking for him. We went to all the usual places where he had gone previously and where we thought he may go but never thought of the IGA. We got a phone call from Nathan's respite centre to say that one of the ladies who used to work with Nathan there was with him at the IGA. It was lucky she was there, since the people who worked there had no idea what to do about this child who wasn't speaking just taking jars of Nutella off the shelf, scooping it out with his fingers and eating it.

Since these incidents I have made up laminated information sheets with Nathans photo and our phone numbers on it and taken it to the places he likes to run away to. Just recently he had run away and Mark went straight away to the IGA while I checked around other places he may have gone. When I got to the IGA Mark was out the back with Nathan and the manager. The manager was so upset, she was actually in tears, she was worried that someone had beaten him up because he had a black eye, which was actually one he had given himself. She said she knew that something else was wrong as well and that he was probably autistic because she has a niece on the spectrum and she does the same sort of things Nathan does like covering his ears at loud sounds or music.

She was apologising for calling the police but she didn't know what else to do. I asked her about the laminated information sheet I had given them. She asked me who I had given it to. I told her I had given it to one of the other female managers and she said there were no other female managers. It clicked then with her that it was actually the previous owners who I had given it to. These new owners didn't know about it. One of the men went to have a look in the office and found it. It was sitting on the desk amongst other paper work. They have since pinned it up on the wall so if he ever does run away they know to ring us straight away.

Nathan has always been a bit of escapee, right from when he was little. When he was only about three he was trying to get to his older brothers, who were playing with their friends out in the street. I had been hanging clothes on the line and I only saw him at the last minute before he fell over our six foot fence. He had dragged one of the Otto bins over to the fence, climbed on in and fell over. I thought he would have done himself some real damage, but he just screamed got up and tried to run off to play with the big boys.

A lot of changes had to be made at Koonawarra School where Nathan attended preschool and kindergarten because of his numerous escape attempts. When he was in preschool they had to put extra tall fences over the stairs to the playground because he would get on the top step and pull himself over the fence and try to escape. When he moved over to kindergarten his classroom was right near the gate, and he used to like to take off out of the classroom sometimes. There was always a worry that if he got out of his classroom he would be able to run straight out onto the road. A tall fence was put in from his classroom across to the fence near the gate, so if he got out of the classroom he couldn't get near the road instead he would run down into the playground. At the school Nathan now attends, there are extra tall fences around each classroom but his teachers still have to be vigilant. If he wants to get out in the playground to jump on the trampoline or demolish a tree, nothing is going to stop him, not even a supposedly escape proof fence.

When Nathan was only two we bought the house we currently live in and I think somehow we must have known then that we would need this house now because it is like a fortress. I call it Fort Knox because we have become like jailers, always vigilant and always having to make sure the doors are all securely locked. It has bars on all the windows and it has extremely solid screen doors.

I don't particularly like being a jailer for my child, but this is what I have had to become to keep him from going and stealing food from the shops and to keep him safe from getting picked up by a paedophile or once again getting hit by a car.

Right from an early age Nathan has been a climber

This is not Nutella but drinking chocolate. There was too much drama from his disappearance that we never got photos of him covered in Nutella but you can imagine how much worse he looked after his Nutella escapades.

THE IMPOSSIBLE PUZZLE

Trying to figure out autism is like trying to do a million piece puzzle and every time you almost get it done someone comes along and knocks all the pieces all over the floor. This is how it has been as I have tried to find help for Nathan. I start something and think it is helping but the effects only seem to help for a very short while.

Throughout the autism journey I have searched many places for answers. I have taken Nathan to seen countless doctors, naturopaths, homeopaths and therapists.

A few years back, in the school holidays, we went to Sydney for a week of intensive therapy at a sensory gym. They did therapeutic listening, deep pressure therapy and play therapy. There was little that we took away from that week that would help Nathan in the long run. The only thing that did any good was the deep pressure techniques, that a lot of kids with autism crave, but it still had no positive effect on his behaviour.

I started taking him to Canberra to see a naturopath who did hand scans that showed what supplements Nathan should be taking and what foods he should be having. It was expensive to keep going there especially when you only saw minimal improvement. It was also very difficult to implement the dietary regime that he was supposed to follow.

We have done food testing through a hospital in Sydney which helped both me and Nathan in our overall health because I did the testing alongside him so I could see what would happen. Although it has helped our health it again did nothing to improve Nathan's behaviour.

I was home on my own with Nathan one weekend and he had been really good and I didn't feel like cooking so I decided that we would have a pizza. I ordered, what I was thinking would be the healthiest, a vegetarian pizza. It wasn't long before I realised that I had made a terrible mistake in letting him have pizza. He went into a rage and before I could get him to his room he had smashed a picture and put more holes in the walls.

We went to friends for a party one night and Nathan went inside. We found him sitting on their lounge and he had eaten almost a whole packet of Eton biscuits from Aldi. We weren't too worried about him eating them until he started to go into one of his meltdowns. He started hitting everything and we had to hold him down so he didn't destroy anything. He kept screaming and kicking and he was so worked up that he started vomiting and he was so hot. As he calmed down a bit my friend ran him a bath and when he got into it, and he cooled down, he started to come back to himself again.

It is really hard to explain to people that food can be a huge problem in their life and having to explain about how food affects Nathan and why I have him on a special diet is a bit difficult because so many people just don't believe that food can be such an issue. I know this is only one of Nathan's issues but it is a big one and even though it is hard to keep him on his diet, especially when he goes to school and respite, it is essential because I have lived with the side effects and they are certainly not pretty.

We have tried many different types of drugs most with little to no effect and some of them have even made his behaviour even worse.

We spent many days going to an occupational therapist and all he ever wanted to do was go on the big swing they had there, and to draw on the white board. The therapist, after a lot of time and patience, was actually able to help him write his number 8's again and that was about as far as we came in all the time we spent going.

We have tried using classical music and therapeutic listening. I suppose there are a lot of things I haven't tried but there are many that I have. However, I just don't seem to get anywhere as far as any benefits to his behavioural issues go.

At the end of the 2014/15 school holidays I was at my wits' end not knowing if I could go on and the following is my journal entry for that day and also the point at which we were directed to get some funding to help us set up the house so it was safer for Nathan and also to get some in home help.

Today 29.1.15 - _the first day of school for many, including my son, Nathan. This was supposed to be a happy day but it has just left me shattered. After much frustration trying to get Nathan ready for school he seemed happy and ready to get onto the bus. At the last minute he wouldn't get on and they told me that they are not allowed to wait for longer than 3 minutes to get him on. As they talked to me and we tried to get him on all the frustrations that have beset us overwhelmed me and the tears started to flow._

After having to drive him to school myself I sit here now and the tears are slowly drying up but the emotions are still very raw. As I sit and contemplate the fact that I may no longer be able to care for my son I feel like

I have failed him. All the "WHAT IF'S" run through my head. WHAT IF I was stronger, WHAT IF I was smarter and could figure out how to help him. The biggest WHAT IF for me is WHAT IF I was more vigilant and never allowed him to get away from me in the shops all those years ago and run out into traffic and get hit by a car. Would he have regressed so far into his autism?

I think back over these holidays and wonder how I made it through the day sometimes. These holidays have seen Nathan smash my TV, put more holes in in his room. While he was in respite he knocked 2 panels out of the fence, broke a couple of windows and smashed his Ipad, the 3ʳᵈ and last because I can't work and we can't afford to keep replacing them and all the other things he has damaged.

This decision, a decision that I have to face up to - whether I can continue to care for him is breaking my heart. For 13 years I have been there for him, as he suffered through his epilepsy, as he tried to fit into school and when he was struck by a car and broke his hip and arm and I have been there as he continues to suffer as a result of that accident.

Battling for all these years has left me exhausted and I no longer know where to turn for help. I have done all I can for him but it just hasn't been enough and no-one can tell me what to do next. My body is a wreck and it won't take much more of the physical altercations that I have to deal with every day. Nathan is getting so big and strong and it can be very scary at times. No parent should be scared of their child.

I have been wishing, hoping and praying that someone or something would come along to help us escape this nightmare but it never happens and the strength that I had is being slowly sucked out of me and the despair has set in. I am still hopeful that a miracle will occur and that my boy doesn't have to continue to suffer!

Not long after I wrote this I saw a Dr Phil show about inflammation in the brain and how it affected the body and how a grain free diet was having positive effects for some people. Nathan was already on a gluten, lactose and preservative free diet but once I took him off the grains altogether there was a marked improvement in his behaviour. In addition to this his dose of medication was put up and when both of these things are kept on an even keel he is a lot better. He still has a lot of behavioural issues but this is the best year he has had in the last four years. Nathan often used to get colds and because he doesn't talk it is hard to know how he is feeling and exactly what the best medicine is to give him. Because I didn't want him, or me, getting sick we started having Turmeric and Ginger every day and since this we haven't been sick.

There is one other thing that I have started recently and I found this is a must for both of us and that is Magnesium baths. I was constantly having a sore back and knees and since I have been having these baths both of these are much better. Since I started these baths again Nathan has taken to lying in the bath for about an hour and he seems to be sleeping better now.

We have just recently taken Nathan out to Cowra to a Naturopath who was worked in Hong Kong and spent many years working with children with autism. He does live blood analysis, and I learnt more from him in ½ an hour than I have from all the doctors I have seen over the last 10 years. We have only just started the treatment and we are hoping we have good results.

I am sure there are many things that I haven't tried but there are many that I have and as long as my boy continues to suffer I will continue to seek answers to this seemingly impossible puzzle.

The many faces of autism

IT'S BEEN AN EMOTIONAL DAY

At the end of some days the only way I seem to be able to put all the emotions aside, so that I can get some sleep, is to write down how I am feeling. As life has gotten tougher with Nathan I have found that I have to do this more and more often. The following are some of the entries from my journal.

2014 - SOMETIME

I thought this life was supposed to be about living but what I am doing is barely existing. The reality I pictured for myself growing up is so distant to what I am living right now. Living life in fear, fear that Nathan is going to really hurt me one day, fear that Nathan is going to really hurt himself, fear that our house is going to become even more of a disaster zone than it already is and fear that I am going to hurt Nathan very badly when he goes into a rage and I try to stop him and my anger goes past the point of no return - No that's not living. The façade I display to the outside world hides a darkness that I dwell in each and every day. The mask I put on each day covers up the tears and trauma that are always close to the surface that if anybody prods a little too hard they will become evident for all to see and I don't want people to feel pity for me so I don't allow people too close to my interior.

24.6.14

Nathan has been in respite since Friday. I went to dancing Friday morning. Friday night we went out for Josh's Birthday. Saturday morning I went dancing. Saturday arvo I spent time with my friend, Rhonda, at the art gallery in Wollongong then hung out with Josh for a while then home for a few drinks. Sunday was Josh's actual birthday so we went to San Churros for brunch then went abseiling. We hung out with Josh at his place with him and his mates. Monday morning I went dancing then had a meeting with Anna Watson (our local member of Parliament) in the afternoon and went to Toastmasters that night.

I packed a lot into my time while he was in respite and to say that I missed him would be a lie. I thought about him quite a lot but most of it was thinking about how easy my life is when he isn't with us. He returns tomorrow and it is with great dread because the hard work begins again.

I love my boy but I continually hope and pray that some day soon he will get easier to handle. I wish he didn't have to suffer the way he does. His suffering not only affects him but it affects our whole family. I just want to crawl into my bed and never get out again. I am emotional now knowing that he comes home tomorrow and the roller coaster starts again. Please let me find a way to help him not only so we can have an easier life but so he can too. He is a beautiful boy and he shouldn't have to suffer the way he does.

25.6.14

Today I am feeling a little sad, NO a lot sad. I just can't seem to lift myself out of this black mood. My petition is not going as well as I would like. Sometimes I feel people really care but today when I've gone into some of the offices the petitions have just gone probably been thrown out. It makes it seems so hard. I wonder if all the effort is going to make a difference or am I just wasting my time because the government is much bigger than I am and they always seems to get their way in the end.

Nathan comes home today after being in respite and straight away we have to take him to the doctor because he may have a urinary tract infection. I am really dreading that because who knows what his behaviour is going to be like.

Another thing that is dragging me down is that I am not sleeping properly from the tension in my life. I just don't feel like doing anything.

5.7.14

Today I am really pissed off. I may as well not be here because nobody listens to me. The reason for my annoyance is yesterday I dropped Mark at the club in the afternoon (2.00pm). He says I won't be long just a couple of beers and I'll be home. We sit around and light the fire, have a few drinks with the boys. Well 6.00pm rolls around, I ring him again and he says "I bought tickets in the raffle". I say OK. I ring him again and he now says "I'm just watching the football it will be over in 10 minutes so I go to pick him up and he's on the pokies. Josh goes in to get him and I sit in the car for ages. It's finally 10.15 and he comes out. As we are driving he says you could drop me and Josh off at the Citizens Bowling Club but I say no.

He said he was staying away from the pokies and I drove home. After agreeing with me it isn't a good idea to go out again he and Josh make a drink and I go to bed. I get up at 1.30 am and they aren't home. I just go back to bed - totally over it. I have no idea what time they got home. Josh is moving to Wollongong today and Mark is going to be useless because he drank too much. One minute he says let's live and not worry about money then he says we need to knuckle down then he goes and wastes it in the pokies.

14.7.14

Tonight the sadness bug has bitten hard. Like a cranky crocodile it has clamped its jaw shut tight and won't let go. There is no particular reason for this. Today has been no harder nor any easier than any other day. I went out for a drive with all three of the boys today and it was good to be out with them but you can't enjoy it totally because there is always that problem of not knowing what Nathan may do. I couldn't even bring myself to let him out of the car when I got lunch. One of the boys had to stay with him because of the hassles of dealing with him while we are waiting is just too much.

I haven't been sleeping particularly well. Even when Nathan is sleeping well which he hasn't the last couple of night, I'm not sleeping. Tomorrow is going to be particularly hard because he is back at school. I have been enjoying not having to get him ready.

Hope I sleep tonight because I feel like an ancient old relic at the moment.

16.7.14

Why does everything have to be so hard? Today I have been more tired than I have ever been. All I wanted to do when I got home from work was to crawl into my bed and not get up again. I don't recall ever being this bone tired. Is it because I'm getting older and I just can't handle things anymore or is there something wrong with me. I'm very forgetful too but I think that may go along with the tiredness. I hope so anyway.

There was one thing I was very grateful for today. When I went to get Nathan off the bus he gave me the sweetest hug. It was just so sweet. Why can't he be like that all the time?

23.7.14

Nathan spent the weekend in respite and once again I made the most of my weekend. I went to dancing on Saturday and went to a play on Sunday and had a relaxing afternoon.

When he came home on Monday he was so happy and excited to be home. We played and cuddled, jumped on the trampoline together. I think he really enjoys his time away from us. It is something different for him. Because of his behaviour there really isn't much we can do together anymore. I can't take him out on my own anymore which makes it very isolating for him and me.

I wish he could have friends like other kids do. He is such a beautiful child at times. It breaks my heart to see him hurt himself the way he does. All I want to do is hug him and make him feel better but I can't even do that for my boy. He deserves so much more. I wish I was better than what I am and could figure out a way to help him.

I have been so tired lately that even getting out and bouncing on the trampoline with him is just too much hard work. He was awake at four o'clock this morning banging on walls. When it was the right time to get up it took me three attempts to get out of bed. Glad that I have a phone with an alarm to wake me up or Nathan just wouldn't get to school and I wouldn't get to work. I really wish I could stay home and run the house and look after Nathan instead of putting up with a crappy boss and trying to stay positive to keep all the plants alive I have to look after. If I had a good boss the job would be a lot better but I really shouldn't complain too much I have a lot of freedom and he is fairly understanding of my situation even if he couldn't organise a chook raffle and can't run a business for shit.

This morning when I was getting ready amid my tiredness things just weren't going right. I was looking for something and all I could think was its disappeared into the void and all I wanted to do was disappear into that void too or go back to bed and sleep for a month. I want to be a bear and hibernate for the winter and only come out when things look better.

I saw something on the TV about a boy being hit by a car and the family got compensation and the boy had therapy and was OK. All I could think was where's my compensation. Nathan got hit by a car and we got squat and his problems are ongoing with no one being able to help him get back to where he can lead any semblance of a normal life.

18.8.14

Today has been a very emotional day for me. After Nathan not going to bed til after midnight and the storm raging all night there was very little sleep to be had. I went to dancing this morning which was, as always, great because it distracts me from the real world.

This afternoon was a visit to Nathan's psychiatrist. As I sat in the waiting room I was on edge and as I entered the room and started to show the doc photos of what Nathan has been doing to himself I was in tears. He went to say I understand how hard it is and that just made me more upset. I got cranky with him and I said "No you don't understand. You can't understand until you have lived what I live with every day". He went on to say that all we can do is try to up his dose of Epilim to see if that will help. Not happy that there isn't any answers for us I left hoping that maybe this medication will help.

Then tonight after yet another email from my idiot boss saying I should be back at work on light duties when there are no light duties on my job I made the decision to quit and I sent in my resignation.

A few wines later and there is relief that I can just be a stay at home mum but there is a worry at the stress that loss of my income will create. I did like my job but when you have a boss who just doesn't care about his staff enough even to ring and ask how they are doing is pretty bad. A boss who doesn't pay your superannuation in over a year, doesn't change the plants (even if they are dead) when you ask who doesn't give you the supplies you need to do your job, who expects you to lie for him to cover his arse, it's just not worth it. I could go on about all the things he does wrong but we could be here for a long time and he just isn't worth the time. It is best to get past it and move on.

I have let the tears roll tonight and as I write they are still close to the surface. I don't cry all that often but on a day like today they become an intermittent waterfall and when they have welled up instead of pushing them back down and hiding them from sight I let them fall unbidden allowing anyone around me to see. The emotion today has been very raw and I'm not sure I can hide that away any longer. I don't want to become some sort of sookie la la but I can't continue to supress the emotion that builds up and causes days like today.

9.11.14

Not only is this a monumental day worldwide but also personally. It has been 13 years since the day I sat in Wollongong Hospital, heavily pregnant, as I watched the announcement that the Twin Towers had collapsed.

Today and this week has seen many highs and lows. Most people have no idea how these highs and lows can affect someone who lives with what I do.

I had a great morning on Tuesday at Toastmasters. I delivered an amazing speech and maybe I got a little overexcited from people's reactions, I don't know, but as I went to put my gear in the car I fell down the stairs once again injuring my damaged shoulder and I hurt my wrist too.

On Wednesday I had to take Nathan to the doctor only to find out that he had broken his own arm somehow. We don't know how or when he did but it had been broken for at least a few days. Nathan had also picked up Scabies as well which he passed on to me. The itch was horrid. So I had to treat Nathan for that then get a cast put on his broken arm.

Today I'm told my first transcription job is good but then I have to deal with Nathan because he is trying to rip his cast off at school. We had to take him back to the physio to repair it before he totally destroyed it. On the way home we had to buy a heap of superglue so he wasn't able to pull the end of the fibreglass up and wreck the cast.

Finally get Nathan organised and settled then off to our local bowling club we go where I host trivia once a fortnight. We had such a great night.

17.9.14

Nathan was awake most the night last night. I was up with him until 1.00 in the morning and when I left him I had hoped he that he was ready to go to sleep but obviously not because his light was on this morning and he had pulled a heap of stuff out of his cupboard to try to find clothes because he had pissed himself. I was absolutely exhausted this morning and I did some washing and some transcription work which I totally stuffed up. When Brendon came home and told me I looked terrible I decided I needed a nanna nap but unfortunately the phone annoyed me a couple of times so I didn't get much rest.

Nathan had a really terrible day at school and I thought I was in for it this afternoon but he got off the bus and gave me a big kiss. He was good most of the afternoon until just before bedtime when he started smacking himself in the face. I put him in his room and he settled fairly quickly and he went to bed without a drama.

29.11.14

Anger is the wind which blows out the lamp of the mind - Robert Green Ingersoll

No truer words have been said than those on a day like today. Waking from another restless sleep has left me feeling -well I don't know - it's hard to explain. I guess it's a mixture of sadness, tiredness but most of all anger. Anger has been ever present and it has certainly blown my candle out today because I feel dark, like it has taken all the joy out of my life and left me feeling cold and lonely. I went about my morning in a kind of zombified state just wishing I could feel better but not being able to drag my mind from the anger that is drowning my thoughts and threatening to drag me under.

Midday came and the exhaustion had taken its toll so I put a movie on with Nathan and we had a nap while Shrek was playing on the TV. When I awoke I felt somewhat better. Not great but I didn't feel that weight of sadness trying to drown me any longer.

Nathan started to meltdown and when I got him to his room Mark went in and yelled at him and when I told him that wasn't a good idea he yelled at me and all that sadness, tiredness and anger hit me like a sledgehammer.

I walked outside to get the washing off the line and instead of being able to unpeg the towels I sat on the ground and cried. Tears that burned my cheeks like hot coals flowing from a volcano. The towels flapped around my head tormenting me as they slapped my face. I closed my eyes and all I could see was red. It was like all that anger that was welled up inside of me would not leave me alone and even when I closed my eyes to try to stop the tears it was taunting me.

So close to the surface is this anger that I can't be around anyone lest I vent my fury on them. I couldn't let Nathan out of his room until he was calm but more so until I was calm enough.

Every time I turn around on social media there are tributes to Phil Hughes and yes I can understand why they are grieving but I grieve every day because my child won't ever experience anywhere near what this guy got to experience in his short life.

I can't write anymore it feels like my mind is in a vice and all the grief and sorrow I live with every day is threatening to clench it so tight that I may no longer be able to function as a normal human being ever again.

30.11.14

This year has been the toughest so far. As Nathan gets bigger and stronger my resolve seems to get weaker. There has always been this hope in me, burning like a bright flame, but that has all but been extinguished. Dampened by the realization that I can't fix him, no one can, I have been overwhelmed with emotions so dark and distressing that some days I can barely function.

All the happiness seems to have been sucked out of me in the last few days and no matter what I just can't feel happy. I see everyone getting ready for Christmas and my despair at my situation gets worse. I hate that I can't do the normal things that everyone else can at this time of year like taking my child to Christmas parties or to the carols.

Sometimes like today I have to really force myself to do things because all I feel like is crawling into my bed and never having to face the crap that is my life again.

1.12.14

After a weekend of feeling like I just want to get in my car and drive off into the sunset and never return to this life I breath a huge sigh of relief this morning as Nathan gets on the bus to school. This is first day of the festive season and I most certainly don't feel festive at all. The joy that December had always brought is no longer there. It is so hard to listen to the radio hearing all the great things that people will be doing over the holidays. I feel like turning the TV and radio off and not turning them back on again. I don't want to know about all the things others are doing that I just can't do. Growing up, even though we were poor, Christmas was always an exciting time. It was a time for family and friends to come together and enjoy just being together. I can't even do that anymore because I just can't take Nathan anywhere because of the destruction he can cause.

30.12.14

Sadness and lethargy are overwhelming me at the moment and it is made all that much worse by all the negativity that I am surrounded by. Today I feel like crawling back into bed and possibly having a cry but I don't have that luxury because I have Nathan. He consumes my existence. It is so hard to feel whole and sane when you are living in a constant state of stress. My bedroom is my hideaway, my sanctuary from a cruel world that continues to inflict its wrath upon me. I've had people say to me why don't I ring them when I'm feeling like this. There are many reasons for not letting people into my tear soaked realm. I have cried so many tears since this child came into my life and my tears are my solace. Usually as they flow I rely on the only person that I have always had to pull me out and that is me.

I don't need people to feel pity for me, that is not in my nature. I don't like to cry in front of people. I don't need my grief to become a spectator sport for people who enjoy seeing other people suffer. In times like this I like to do what I do best and that is write down how I'm feeling and as the ink flows the tears start to dry up.

Although some days like today when I am stuck at home with Nathan the days seem to draw on and on and I face many challenges with very few rewards. When they do come they are so much sweeter. Just those little moments when Nathan comes up and puckers up and gives me one of his big smoochy kisses can be OH so special.

At the moment Nathan is lying on the lounge looking at a book and it feels nice to take a breather for a few moments but still not knowing when the next tantrum or meltdown will occur is straining on the nerves.

I often wonder what my life would be like if I didn't have Nathan or if he was a normal kid. Would I be as appreciative of those special moments or would I just become another blast person wandering aimlessly through this life. Has he been given to me for a specific purpose? If there is a reason I would certainly like to know because at the moment I'm feeling lost. I've tried so hard to help him but I feel like I'm in some kind of labyrinth and no matter which way I turn I can't find the exit from this crazy maze.

6.3.15

It's been a while since I've written about how I've been feeling. Emotions are raw most days and all I want to do is open up and allow the tears to fall. Tears that will fall like a waterfall if I let them but that is not who I am, not who I was taught to be. I was never taught to show emotion and if I cried I was being a sook, a wuss or some other weak willed person but tonight all I want is to cry.

Why the tears?

- *Because my boy is misunderstood not only by everyone around him but mostly because me (his mother) has no way to help him, no way to reach into his realm and make his life better*

- *Because this life is so isolating. Sometimes I just want to walk out the front door and keep walking and never look back. To find a new way to live that is filled with family, friends, laughter and joy.*

- *Because I just want to feel loved. This is a hard one to explain but my entire life has been filled with struggle and torment that all I want is to be made to feel special.*

- *Because every day there seems to be something breaking down and because I can't work it is just one more thing to weigh me down. Not having enough money to live comfortably and knowing I could be working if it wasn't for Nathan is extremely difficult.*

- *Because I don't sleep well at night due to all that stress weighs on me and sometimes it feels like I have a weight sitting on my chest, like a bomb ticking away waiting to go off. The weight on my chest is not just a metaphor but an actual physical feeling that some days I wonder if the stress is causing some internal physical damage that I don't realise. I fight so hard to be strong because I know my boy needs me but can I continue this way.*

- *Because I know there is more within me that I can contribute to our world but most days it takes all my effort just to make it through the day.*

- *Because I'm lonely*

- *Because this life feels more like a burden than a blessing. I want to inspire people not drag them down into the despair that sometimes overwhelms me and causes me to wish that the ground would open up and swallow me.*

The complexities of my life, past and present, are of a nature that people should not have to deal with - EVER. The conflict that I grew up with, and even more so now, makes you truly ponder what this life is about. As a child I had no choice as to how I lived and what I lived seems like some kind of dream and I wonder if it was really as rough as I thought it was. It was just life and I carried on with it every day taking it as it came. Most of the time I felt misplaced, like I wasn't important, like it didn't matter if I existed or not, like no one would miss me. One thing that I never contemplated was leaving this life because I have always had hope that things would get better. I still feel like this. Even in the depths of my despair, there has and I hope always will be, a hope that things will get better.

Opting out of this life because it is too tough has never been an option. It doesn't mean I haven't thought about it though. I think every person in my situation would think about it at some stage. I guess there is a fighting spirit within me that pushes me and when things get rough I get tough.

It has been hard with all the physical injuries that I have had to deal with lately but one thing I can't do is give up. I can't give up on myself, no matter how much pain I am in and I can't (no matter how many people tell me I should) give up on my boy. He is a part of me and I will fight with him and for him until I have nothing left to give, until all the strength ebbs from my body and I pass from this life to next I will fight. I will fight because that is what I was taught to do, by my family circumstance, by the bullies, by the knocks and the hard times. I was taught to fight and fight I will.

IT'S A KNOCKOUT

Nathan was supposed to be in respite for a full weekend one time but come Sunday I got a phone call to say I had to go and pick him up because he had injured one of the staff.

When I got out there I found out that he had more than injured her. He had actually knocked her out and put her teeth through her lip. She had already been taken to the hospital when I got there. I saw her some time later and she said that while she was being taken care of Nathan was coming up to her to try and be affectionate. After his meltdown he may have realised what he had done and was trying to show her that he didn't mean to do what he had done to her.

She moved on to another job working at the hospital after this incident, but I spoke to her recently and she said that she missed the job and all of the kids, even Nathan.

Nathan hasn't been able to do any sort of extra curricula activities for a long time due to his behaviour. I was so excited this year when he had calmed down enough on his new diet and medication to be able to start doing some activities with him again.

I took him to Riding for the Disabled up at Fitzroy Falls, which is almost an hour's drive up the mountain, because the centre which is closest to us has closed. This was the first time he has ridden in three years. He enjoyed being back on the horse but the session wasn't long enough and he didn't like stopping all the time. He just wanted to go fast. He had the biggest smile when they gave him a little trot and he was almost jumping in the saddle to get the horse to go fast again. They couldn't trot him too much because he was in an arena with many other children who are less able than he is. The whole time, including when they trotted him, he didn't hold onto the saddle or reins at all. They were astounded at how good his balance was. As they get to know him and how capable he is on a horse I am hoping that they will be able to take him out and give him a bit more freedom to go faster.

At the end of his class one of the ladies came up to me and said that Nathan had nearly caused her to shed a tear. I said I know what you mean, I was a bit like that myself because before he got off the horse he leant forward wrapped his arms around her neck and gave her the biggest cuddle.

When we came back to Wollongong I gave him some lunch and took him in to the hospital to get his blood tests done. He was surprisingly good as we waited with our Life Without Barriers worker who came along to lend a hand. It still took four of us to hold Nathan but he didn't struggle as much as some other times when he has had to have blood drawn.

His behaviour had been exceptional all throughout the day but it took a dramatic turn about five o'clock though, whether he was hungry or thirsty, I don't know or maybe it was both. I think he may have been dehydrated because he hadn't had a drink since breakfast and they did have to take quite a bit of blood for all the tests he needed. He went into a meltdown really fast and when I tried to stop him smashing things on my desk and from biting himself he head-butted me in the face. I am usually pretty good at knowing his behaviour and being able to get out of his way but I was caught off guard because he hadn't had a meltdown like this in a very long time. He didn't knock me out but I think it came very close. When I fell on the ground he punched me in the back. I got up and blood was pouring out of my nose.

He ran up the hall in the direction of his room and he went to hit the wall but I chased him into his room. He hit and elbowed the walls, kicked his bed. I shut him in his room and I sat on the floor in the hall outside his room with my head in my hands in pain and with tears rolling down my face listening to him as he laid into the walls in his room.

As soon as my vision cleared and I felt stable enough I got up to get some medication that would calm him down.

After he had calmed enough I bought him out and gave him his other medication that he has to have in the afternoon with a couple of cups of water and his dinner. I was crying as I gave him his tablets and he looked at me and he started crying too. That is the first time I have seen any sort of empathy from him. Sometimes he cries immediately after he has a meltdown but this time it only seemed to happen when he saw me crying.

Josh rang a little while later to have a chat and he could hear in my voice that something was wrong. As I told him what had happened I started to cry again and he got his housemate to drive him out to check on me.

While I was talking to Josh he noticed something on the floor and picked it up. It was the unicorn pendant I had been wearing. In the turmoil I didn't even realise that it had even been pulled off. We couldn't find my necklace though. It wasn't until I was getting ready to go to bed that I found it caught up in my clothes.

I talked with Josh and Phil for a while and when I sat on the lounge Nathan came over and sat next to me and he snuggled in. He was loving and cuddly and it is so hard to believe that he could have had such a moment of utter madness.

For weeks after this incident I continued to have headaches and it felt like I had a bad sinus infection. It is lucky for me that I don't bruise easily or I would probably have ended up with two black eyes.

Sometimes after one of Nathan's meltdowns I feel like a human punching bag. During the meltdown because senses are heightened, mostly adrenalin, I don't feel the blows. Once it's over and the adrenalin ebbs away, it's then I feel every blow that was inflicted. I know, like when my Dad hit me, that is not him and not what he wants to do. After he has calmed down, and he comes for a snuggle it is so hard to believe that only moments before he was trying to beat the life out of me. How could I be upset with him when he just doesn't seem to be able to control himself and is so loving and affectionate afterwards.

I never can tell when he is going to go into a meltdown. Nathan is getting so big now and if these meltdowns continue with as much ferocity as they have I may not get up again.

Look Ma no hands!
Great therapy with the horses at
Riding for the Disabled.

Nathan having cuddles with beautiful Millie

I DON'T KNOW HOW YOU DO IT

As you can see from the previous chapters the life I live is not a particularly easy one and if I had a dollar for every time someone said to me "I don't know how you do it" the mortgage would be well and truly paid off and I if I had a dollar for every time someone even though it I would be living on easy street. I would probably be sitting on some tropical island sipping cocktails with sexy cabana boys fanning me and feeding me grapes. One can but dream!

I was talking to someone who has a child, with autism, that is five years younger than Nathan and she asked me how we lived at home. I said "we don't live we exist - JUST!". We live each day hoping that someday, somewhere, someone will be able to help Nathan. I personally live for his next respite stay and if for some reason he can't go because of injury or illness I am devastated. I live most days in a constant state of exhaustion some days seemingly on auto-pilot. At the end of those days I flop on the couch and look back on the day and wonder. I wonder at the cruelty that life can deal out. Not only for us as a family but for Nathan who has to live his life in this constantly agitated state.

I often think that no one prepared me for this but that is quite the contrary because when I really think about it I have been training for this all my life. The difficulties that I lived through in my youth, the courses I have done, the jobs I have had, the people who are and have been a part of my have all helped prepare me for what I live with in the here and now.

Brendon and Josh are two very important people in mine and Nathan's life. They have had a lot to deal with because of the way Nathan is, but they have always been a great help to me. They are so much stronger than me and there have been so many times that they have had to help me with Nathan because I just don't have the strength. Even though Mark and I are not together we still share this house because of Nathan and if I need him to help when Nathan is having issues he will help me out.

I did a Visual Arts course in 2009/10 which has been very helpful when I have had to come up creative solutions to problems that have come along. Being creative and thinking outside the box has been a necessity when it comes to life with Nathan. Some of my creativity, I think, comes from genes. My mum is an amazing sewer, as are my sisters. One of them is great at embroidery and the other does amazing crochet. I on the other hand, tend to be erratic and slightly schizophrenic when it comes to my creative pursuits. I can't seem to stick to one project for very long. One day I might be drawing, the next painting, beading, mosaicing or making concrete stepping stones, whatever takes my fancy when I am in the creative mood.

My creativity has had to come to the fore in so many ways most of these are coming up with ways to stop Nathan from destroying things whether it's figuring out a way to stop him pulling his curtains down and destroying the curtain rods, to fixing his bed so he can't knock it to pieces or doing art works that I can use to put over all the holes he has created in the walls.

Another part of my life that taught me to be flexible was moving constantly when I was growing up. We moved from Grenfell to Forbes while I was in second class. Throughout the rest of my schooling (2nd class to Year 10) we moved six times. In that time we lived on a farm for a number of years and that was a time where you had to be versatile to do the work on the farm, from caring for the animals (the pigs were my chore after school) but I also loved the goats and the chickens. The geese were interesting creatures. One day they were friendly the next they would try to bite your finger off with their raspy bills. Shearing time was always fun, from throwing the fleeces on the sorting tables to jumping in the bales of wool to squash them.

Scouting was another massive learning period in my life. This is where I really learnt to be an adult but also how to really enjoy being a big kid. Organising camps and taking the kids into the bush taught me some much needed organisational skills that were somewhat lacking before I came into the scouting movement. The Scouting motto is "BE PREPARED" and I have certainly had to be prepared for so many different situations that have come along with Nathan.

Camping has long been a part of my life and I still love getting out in the great outdoors. Our fishing crew went down to Burrinjuck Dam for a weekend and as we sat around the fire we decided that we should come up with a name for ourselves. As we talked about our lives we came up with the name "The Outcast Crew" for two reasons none of us really liked or fitted into school and we always felt on the outer and when we went camping we were <u>out</u> to fish and <u>cast</u> our lines in the water.

On one of our trips to Shoalhaven Heads we had some pretty nasty weather. I had packed up my tent because the guys had gone to the pub and I had had enough of dealing with Nathan on my own so I was going to go home. They came back and convinced me to stay so I slept in the tent that was still set up. I can't say I actually got any sleep because it was blowing a gale and it rained all night. At about 3 in morning our tent started to fill with water and had blown over. We raced out of our tents and pulled out the power cords so we didn't end up electrocuted. I grabbed Nathan and I knew that the back windows of the BBQ hut was never locked so I slid it open and literally threw him in the window and told him to stay in there. I was left without my rain coat because someone else had put mine on. Our first priority was to secure the gazebo that was trying to fly away. I was absolutely saturated and every time I bent down to grab something by pyjama pants would fall down. It was a good thing that all the lights had gone out. After that trip our friend who is a little older than us had decided that we would not be camping again but we did. We went back to the same place and once again it rained all weekend It wasn't as nasty as before so all we could do was sit around in the BBQ hut and play cards or go to the club. That really was the last straw when it came to camping for him so we started going cabining instead.

Before Nathan was born I started a six month work opportunities for women course at Yallah Tafe in horticulture. I got a job at Hardware House (now Bunnings) from doing the course. I went on to do the three year Certificate III course. Nathan's arrival occurred about halfway through my studies but I continued on and finished the course. Going back to formal study was a hard thing because all through school I hated to study. I put a lot of effort into my course and by doing really well it gave me a great sense of accomplishment. I unfortunately had to give up this job once Nathan came along. I am really glad that I am a gardener because Nathan loves to be out in my garden.

Life with an autistic child can become very isolating and I am not a person who does well in isolation, so I have to do things that will help to stave it off.

One of these is Toastmasters (public speaking). I started this a few years ago and that has been an outlet that I have really enjoyed mostly because I like to talk and because it has given me a way to voice what I deal with on a day to day basis. This has also given me the confidence to get up and speak at the rallies and meetings that I go to in relation to the closure of Nathan's respite centre.

It also gave me the confidence to take on something that I really love doing. I now host trivia at our local bowling club once a fortnight. It is great being Trivia Master and having all the answers. I have played a few times but I am not the most intelligent person so I can't contribute much to a team but I can talk and I really enjoy when the teams give me a bit of cheek because I give it straight back to them.

There are quite often questions or words that I may come across with some sexual connotations and there is often lots of crude comments. I have had a couple of nights that I was laughing so hard that I struggled to get the questions out. The best thing is that there is always lots of laughter.

"I love people who make me laugh. I honestly think it's the thing I like the most, to laugh. It cures a multitude of ills. It's probably the most important thing in a person." AUDREY HEPBURN

GET YOUR GROOVE ON

There is one other thing that I do and this thing deserves its own chapter because it is my most favourite thing. It helps me cope with the day to day struggles. Twice a week I go to therapy A.K.A. Linedancing. The following is a letter that I wrote to my linedance teachers and I think it says it all about how I feel to be part of the linedance community.

To Tom, Donna and Maddy

I could not be prouder to say that I am a linedancer especially with your club. Coming here every week makes my life bearable.

After Nathan was struck by the car in 2010 my life has been filled with drama and sadness bought on by the violent out-of-control rages that has left my life in tatters.

The life I lead with my son is a very isolating one especially as I was the youngest of 5 children with none of my siblings living anywhere near me. I miss being a part of that family unit but when I walk into "The Barn" I feel that bond that you can only have with family.

I have been coming to dancing for over 10 years. When I started I was, I'm sad to say, obese but I found a new joy and a wanting for a healthier life through dance. With that in mind and a new found confidence I fought my demons to get back to a very healthy weight with a new vitality for life.

To say the least the last 5 years have been the hardest of my life and if not for being able to come to "The Barn" I would probably cease to function as a normal human being.

Some days it is extremely hard just to get out of bed without then having to deal with Nathan and get him off to school. By the time I get to dancing I am, very often, not sure if I can even dance. Getting on the dance floor with amazing people around me who laugh WITH ME when I am a total mess and my feet just don't want to do the right thing is just what I need on those days.

People often ask me where I am going and I say <u>therapy</u> A.K.A. Linedancing because no matter what crap has gone down at home I always feel better after I have been to "The Barn".

All I can say is THANK YOU, THANK YOU, THANK YOU for being the amazing people that you are and giving us a place that is so special to so many of us.

Keep on Dancing, Sonia Facey

Everyone needs something in their life that they are truly passionate about and for me that is dancing. Apart from my family this is the most important thing in my life. Dancing makes me a better parent not only because it keeps me fit and healthy but it also makes me happy. In the school holidays when I can't go to dancing because I have to stay at home with Nathan I get very depressed.

If you don't have something in your life that you are truly passionate about and enjoy you need to find it because it will make your life better.

As you can see I have done and do a lot of different things and all these things have combined to make me who I am and how I am able to handle the situation that I have been dealt.

Getting excited to hit the dance floor at one of our Australia Day socials

HEARTACHE AND PAIN

"In my life there's been heartache and pain. I don't know if I can face it again" - FOREIGNER

Not only have I had to deal with the heartache of watching my boy suffer through the pain of his injuries and disability I have also had to deal with the heartache of my marriage falling apart.

Mark and I had been married for 25 years. In that time we have been separated a number of times. Even though we grew up in the same town we grew up very differently. Each with our own set of challenges.

Mark was raised by his grandmother from the age of 18 months when his parents separated. He virtually grew up as an only child whereas I had two older brothers and two older sisters. Mark lived all his life in town but we lived in and out of town.

We moved around a fair bit because Mum was always trying to find the perfect place where she could raise us five kids and where she thought our Dad would be happy and stable. I guess the way we grew up never set us in good stead to have a normal relationship.

There are two main issues, for me, that have caused our relationship to fail. The first is our differences.

- When it comes to weekends or holidays Mark prefers the more leisurely pursuits such as sitting back watching TV or going fishing. I prefer to be more active going bush walking, jogging on the beach, abseiling, swimming, bike riding and dancing.

- I love my garden and try to get out in the garden as much as I can but Mark's only interest in the garden is doing the lawn when it absolutely needs to be done. He has often said that he would prefer the yard was all concrete.

These are just a couple of examples of the differences between us but there are many more. When there are so few common bonds I found that I have drifted away from Mark. As the years have gone on these differences have become more pronounced and I have found myself wanting to do less and less with him and wanting to do more with friends who have common interests to myself.

The other issue is anger and there has been a lot of that in our marriage. During our arguments things have been said that I have really taken to heart at times. I am a very feeling person and it takes a lot to recover from the words that are often regretted later on. There comes a time when you have to say enough is enough, this is not working, we can't go on like this and you have to walk away.

Before we were ever married there were red flags that our relationship was not what it should have been. There was a huge argument the week before the wedding, and friends who were concerned about me, asked me if I was really sure that I wanted to get married. I was very young, naïve and ever the optimist and always believed in the "happily ever after". Being so naïve I always believed that when we did fall apart and things had calmed down that we could make it work. It has taken me a very long time to realise that we just don't seem to be able to make each other happy, and we really are not suited as a couple.

When I am with friends, hosting trivia, dancing or just being by myself at the beach I am a very happy person. When I walk into our house that changes because there has been so much tension between us and it doesn't seem to take much to trigger another disagreement.

Like the song says *"I want to know what love is"* but for me to be able to move on while I have Nathan to care for will be a very difficult road. Although Mark and I are leading very separate lives we still share the house because of Nathan and it will be very awkward to start any sort of relationship.

I could never imagine expecting another man to take on all the issues that I have with Nathan. I won't ever give up on the idea of falling in love. I don't want to live the rest of my life without love, because I have a lot to give, and would love to be able to receive as much in return. For the here and now it is pretty much an impossibility to have any semblance of a normal relationship.

THE BRIGHT SIDE

"Always look on the bright side of life" - Eric Idle

This is another one of my motto's and while I write this chapter the song is stuck in my head. I try to live by this motto and I say try because there are times when it seems there is nothing bright around me. Then these little moments of joy will appear like the rays of the sun peeking through the clouds to allow a little bit of brilliance through. It is these moments of brilliance that I have to hold on to and cherish when the times get tough.

No matter how things are going for me, I look at my life and, I know there are always people who are worse off than I am. Apart from some aches and pains I am fit and healthy. I love life and getting out with family and friends, having a laugh, being in the outdoors and going dancing are all things that make life that much brighter.

The following is another of my journal entries and even though I start off with the negatives of Nathans issues it finishes with the brighter side of his nature, and this is the side of my boy that I cherish.

2014 - SOMETIME

I am always writing stories, poems, speeches about my own feelings but lately I have been thinking about how Nathan must feel.

His frustration levels far outweigh anything I have ever come across. After he got hit by the car and losing his ability to communicate we've seen this happy boy has descend into a state of frustration that sends him into episodes of such self-injurious behaviour that no professional boxer could inflict on someone and not knock them out. I have seen him hit walls so hard I have no idea how he doesn't break bones.

He must be scared because of the confusion and frustration. All I want to do is hold him and let him know that everything is going to be OK but most of the times he doesn't want to be hugged especially if he is in a rage.

I often wonder if he is lonely. His only friends are the adults who look after him and his brothers. I guess the boys in his class could be called his friends, but he only sees them at school.

He can't join a sports group or any of the other extra-curricula activities that other children enjoy.

As I am writing this part I am in tears because it is heart-breaking seeing all these other children enjoying their special activities like going to the zoo, playing at the park, having sleepovers with their friends and your child can't enjoy any of that because of this stupid bloody autism.

When he is happy it makes me happy. Everyone who meets him and sees his smile say that he has the most amazing cheeky smile. His eyes light up the room. He loves staring in my eyes and sometimes it feels like he is looking right into my soul. There in that moment I see my beautiful, special child in a way that no one else can.

I just wish that he could understand the love I have for him and the hope that I have that one day he will be free from the pain that his body causes him.

I adore it when he is in a smoochy mood. He will pucker up his lips and expects you to give him a kiss. Sometimes when you go to give him one he will turn away and laugh. Other times he just gives you the most amazing sloppy kisses and you can't help but feel his love. He can be very cuddly too even though his bear hugs get a little rough at times. I still revel in those special moments, they compensate for all the rough times

There is a truly joyous side to him as well when it comes out it is something to behold because no matter who is around him when he is in one of these moods you can't feel anything but joy. He has a laugh that is so infectious that you just can't help but join in with him.

That is where my hope lies in knowing there are these beautiful sides to him and that one day the harsher side of his nature will abate and my boy won't be quite so tormented as he is at the moment.

When people who know me but don't know what I live with find out about the struggles I go through in my daily life they are amazed that I can be so happy. I have had people say to me that they had no idea what I live with because I always seem so happy. I tell them I am happy because I choose to be happy.

ENJOYING THE WATER

*Burrinjuck Dam - after everyone was tired of continually swimming after him we tied him on a
very long rope to his lifejacket but when he got to the end he tried to chew threw it*

Enjoying the slide at Hawkesbury Riverside Tourist Park

Smooching with his favourite teddy - Bear in the Big Blue House

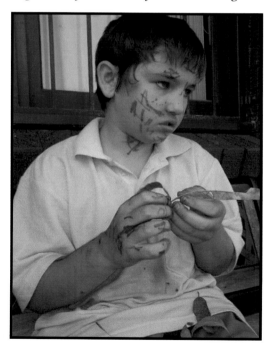

Nathan found a white board marker at school and decided to do some personal art work.

QUE SERA

Que sera, sera - "whatever will be, will be!"

As I said earlier in "Heartache & Pain" my marriage fell apart and it seems we have just became another statistic because the statistics say that 80-90% of marriages with a child with autism won't survive. Come what may between Mark and myself we will forever have a connection due to our boys. Hopefully because of the connection we have we can find a way to put all the past animosities aside and forge a friendship so that we can be there for our boys.

Even though my marriage failed I have learnt a lot along the way. I know that within a marriage, especially if you have a child with a disability, you have to have immense patience with each other and with your child, you need to be empathetic and most of all you need to make each other feel special and loved. You have to laugh together and you have to hold each other up through the hard times.

I know that can be hard for any relationship when times get tough but it is even more important when you have a child with a disability. These special children may not seem like they can pick up on things but I can assure you they can sense more than you will ever realise so be kind to each other and in so doing you are being kind to your child.

In every life there can be a certain amount of pain but it is about how you deal with it that counts. It can leave you bitter and angry or you can learn from it and become a better person. I can at times get very angry, I'm sure most of us can, but I won't allow it to take a hold of my life and cause pain for others.

Living with a child with a disability has not all been bad. It has changed every aspect of my life from the way I live to the way I view the people I meet along the way. I don't automatically think, when I meet someone, they must have a great life because the people that are happiest in this life are often the ones who are living and have lived through the cruellest of times. I know this not only because I am of those people but because I have had the delight of spending time with people in similar circumstances to me and they know the benefit of making the most out of every special moment that comes their way.

When I was little I was such a dreamer and always believed that I would live my fairy tale but that was just childhood fantasy. The fairy tale that I dreamed would be when I was little was never meant to be for me.

I'm not too old to be a dreamer but my dreams are very different from when I was young. The dream I really want to come true is to find a way to help my boy so he can be happy.

I have poured a lot of emotions into this book and I know a lot of it has been painful and if you have taken anything from it I hope it is that you can't dwell in the darkness of someone else's illness. You have to find the things in this life that will make you feel good. You need to be with positive people, love the people you are with, do something caring for someone else every day and most of all choose to be happy.

I still have a long way to go on my journey, I hope, and who knows what is going to come my way, hopefully good things for my boy and me. All I have to left say is Que sera, sera.

Printed in the United States
By Bookmasters